My Mother

MW00917403

My Mother's BiPolar, So What Am I?

Table of Contents

ACKNOWLEDGEMENTS

This book never would have been written had it not been for the abundance of support and love I received throughout the experience. First of all, thank you, Cyndie, for being my sister and best friend. You have been a great example of perseverance and I love you! Of course, thank you, Mom, for your unending support and willingness to help others through your own difficult experience—even though it was not always flattering. You are one of my heroes and I am grateful that you are my mother. Dad, you have always supported all my endeavors, including this book—thank you so much for your encouragement and unconditional love. Thanks to April and Ashley for being such great nieces and for trying to keep me cool. It's a tough job!

Thank you, Sally, for your unending love, support, and patience. I am grateful to you for the hours of editing and for listening to my stories—over and over again. You have been a fantastic spiritual guide along this healing journey. You are a wonderful gift in my life and I love you immensely.

Yvonne, I couldn't have written this book without you. God had a hand in bringing us together to work on this project. You are a gifted writer and a treasured friend! Thank you for making an overwhelming task seem easier and natural. Thank you, Linda, for being such a great editor. You helped make this book the best that it could be.

Janet, what can I say but "Wow!" Thank you so much for creating a powerful piece for the book cover. You are my dear friend and favorite artist.

To my family of friends—Loree, P, Leigh, Camellia, and

Joann—you saw me through the process and provided many hours of encouragement. Thank you so much for being you! Maryann, I suppose it should come as no surprise that your insight and words were the catalyst for this book. I am very grateful for your friendship and your incredible gift!

Bro Bear, you rock! I cherish our late night conversations and look forward to many more.

How can I possibly thank those who shared their stories for this book—including my brother, David. You are all brave people for whom I have great respect and love. Your willingness to contribute will help many people begin to heal and to shift our current way of thinking. My most heartfelt thanks to all of you.

FOREWORD

With clarity and conviction, Angela Grett describes life as the child of a bipolar parent. Angela's deeply moving narrative is an inspiration to us all. With tremendous courage, she faced the pain of her mother's illness and transformed her life.

Bipolar Disorder is so misunderstood, often misdiagnosed and untreated. This highly personal account will help facilitate healing for children of bipolar parents and will be very useful for use in support groups and treatment programs.

Like many adults with Bipolar Disorder, Angela's mom was highly functional. But like adult children of Bipolar, Angela felt the impact of unhealthy boundaries and lack of balance in life.

Angela provides a sound clinical overview of Bipolar Disorder and treatment options. But this book provides so much more. This well written narrative paints vivid portraits of lives of people just like her, who emerged as Children of Bipolar Parents. If you are the child of a bipolar parent, this is a must read! You will be empowered to discover your own gifts and lead a more fulfilling life.

Likewise, this book will empower any child of a parent with any mental or emotional disorder. Angela's is a story of courage, a life of triumph.

Mary F. Zesiewicz, M.D.
Board Certified Psychiatrist

INTRODUCTION

My mother's bipolar. Wow! I said it! If you have a bipolar parent, you realize how difficult it is to make that statement. The stigma that goes with mental illness can be demoralizing. Our society often lumps people with bipolar disorder (or manic/depression) into categories similar to schizophrenia. As a result, we have only recently heard people talk about this subject.

It used to be that any mention of mental illness would conjure up images of straight jackets and padded cells. Thanks to celebrities like Patty Duke, Carrie Fisher, Jane Pauley, Linda Hamilton, and Ted Turner we can now associate well-known faces with this mysterious disease called bipolar disorder. Who would have thought that these hugely successful people have dealt with these same challenges?

Recently, I met a woman named Cathi and we began to talk about our mothers. The conversation began with a mutual roll of the eyes and heavy sighs. We talked about how difficult it was to have any kind of relationship with our mothers because of their behavior. It turned out that her mother was bipolar also. We stayed up talking nearly all night. It was such a relief to be able to share the frustrations and stories about our families and our lives. Shortly after that conversation, I began to realize how little the subject of bipolar was discussed—by people who had the disease. Their families certainly weren't talking about it! I decided to write this book to help the children of those living with bipolar disorder—whether or not they have been diagnosed. This book contains my memories and those from more than a dozen people that I interviewed. My hope is that by reading stories from other families, you will feel a connection and know that you are not alone. After seeing the disorder from an adult child's perspective, you may be able to have a healthier relationship with your bipolar parent and recognize the effect your parent's illness has had on your life.

My intention with this book is *not* to blame our parents for the difficulties we might have experienced as adults. Despite our challenges, we are adults and we benefit by taking responsibility for our behavior and our own lives. I don't mean to create a pity party for all of us poor children of bipolar parents, but I do want to open a dialog and encourage you to talk about your experience. Your parent may have an illness that requires patience, love, and understanding, but it doesn't require you to give up your life and your dreams in order to take care of them. You can face these challenges and still have a healthy relationship with yourself and your parent.

If you are a parent who has been diagnosed with bipolar disorder, my intention in writing this book is *not* to, in any way, disrespect or minimize your experience. Yours is a very difficult journey and one that you likely have not made alone. Your parents, children, significant others and friends have loved you and witnessed your pain. They may not have understood your behavior and perhaps were not supportive. By sharing our experiences, we can begin to understand the mystery of this disorder. In turn, perhaps we will take better care of ourselves and be better equipped to help you get the care that you need.

Although a wide range of readers may be able to relate to experiences shared in the book, my primary objective is to help people realize the impact of growing up with a bipolar parent. If you can look honestly at your own situation and behaviors born out of that experience, you may be able to improve your relationships and your life. Because information leads to understanding, you may be able to reconnect with your mother or father.

I believe there are many people who are suffering with this illness because they have not been diagnosed. Some of the stories may strike a chord with you even though you don't know anyone who has been diagnosed with bipolar disorder.

You may be able to help someone by simply being aware of the information in this book.

You may be wondering why I used the acronym CBP (Child of a Bipolar Parent) after my name. As I began to research books already written about this topic, I noticed a lot of letters after the authors' names (e.g. PhD, MD, PsyD). The credentials intimidated me a bit because I'm certainly no expert on matters of mental illness. My professional experience consists of twenty years in the corporate world. The CBP acronym reminds me that my expertise comes from my first-hand knowledge of being the child of a bipolar parent—the very topic of this book. Clinical information presented here has been researched. My words, however, are from my own experiences and from others who've had similar experiences.

Join me on a journey of understanding a very challenging, mysterious disease called bipolar disorder. Say "good-bye" to your current perception of people who live with this illness. As you begin to learn more about it, you will let go of your frustration and resentment towards your parent. You will begin a wonderful healing journey that will, if nothing else, provide a few "ah-ha" moments. As you read the pages of this book, please know that I am opening my heart to you. Together, we can make the journey easier.

To Mom – thanks for an incredible ride, for your unconditional love, and for not giving up!

To all children of bipolar – you survived – now it's time to thrive!

PART ONE

THE JOURNEY

Chapter 1

Family Memories

My Memories

It could have been raining, snowing, or hailing in Houston, Texas that day in August 1965—who knows? For me, the sky was falling. For reasons that are still unclear to me, my father packed up our things and moved me to his hometown—a four-hour drive from the only world I had ever known. I had just celebrated my fourth birthday and I felt very small sitting between my father and great uncle trying desperately to grasp what was happening. Mommy wasn't coming with us. How does a four-year-old understand something like that?! I can only remember being confused and turning numb. The horror of losing my mother was too much to feel. I was terrified that I would never see her again.

There is some confusion as to how much time lapsed before my mother followed us. It may have been a few days (according to Mom) or several weeks (according to Dad). No matter—that time was filled with fear, sadness and some acting out for me. Since my father worked during the day, I stayed with my great-aunt. My aunt was always loving and gentle, but she expected children to behave and obey their elders. The only time she ever laid a hand on me was when she spanked me for sassing back at her. She felt terrible the moment it happened, but clearly she was dealing with a child who was having a very traumatic experience. I just wanted my mommy back and for things to be "normal" again.

Being separated from my mommy not knowing when or if I would ever see her again was terrifying for me. Fortunately, she did come back, and I was completely elated when I saw her pull into the driveway at my aunt's house. My world had been turned upside down and I would never be the same, but my mommy was back!

I lost the rest of my childhood after Mom and Dad reconciled. That's not to say that I never played or had fun again, but my idea of fun changed. Instead of pretending to "play" house with my toys, I pulled up a chair to the real kitchen sink and helped wash dishes when I was four years old. I truly believed that if I took good care of my mommy, she would never go away again. My personal needs and my ability to voice those needs simply vanished.

When I was preschool age, I had a blue blanket that was an essential comfort for me. I loved to feel the soft satin edging on the blanket. I sucked my thumb as I fell asleep while rubbing the satin on my face. One day my grandmother took the blanket while I slept so she could wash it. I'm sure this precious blanket was in dire need of cleaning, but when I awoke and found the blanket gone, I was hysterical. My grandmother quickly told me that she had washed my blue "blankey" and that it was hanging on the clothesline to dry. I needed the comfort of that blanket so badly that I went outside and stood under the clothesline with that satin edging to my face until I calmed down. I never really thought about the implications of this story until I shared it with a friend. It hit me that such an intense need for comfort from an inanimate object meant that I was not getting all that I needed from the traditional source of comfort—my mommy. I don't mean to imply that she was cold and uncaring. In fact, she cared for me very much and I knew that. She worked very hard to be a good mother. This incident and my need for that blanket, however, raised questions about my inability to reach out to my mother for comfort.

From the time I was seven years old, I felt like I didn't fit in. I thought it was because we practiced a religion that most people didn't understand. We belonged to a Christian faith that chose to celebrate Old Testament holy days. While the rest of my family was exchanging Christmas gifts and hunting for Easter eggs, my sister, bother, and I were observing the Sabbath on Saturday and celebrating our own holidays. We were not allowed to receive Christmas gifts from our family members. This didn't go over very well with my grandparents. Of course, since we did not celebrate Christ's birthday, we also did not honor our own birthdays. I'm not looking for sympathy. It's simply the reality in which I was raised. Things have changed and we all (including my mom) now joyously celebrate birthdays, Christmas and Easter!

I had always been outgoing and very congenial from the time I could walk and talk. After I began attending the church school, my demeanor changed significantly. I soon became a shy, awkward child. I don't believe that my mom's intention was to alienate us from the rest of society; however, her decision to raise us in a very different religious environment did set us apart. I believe that Mom's need for structure in her life came from the chaotic state that she constantly felt. The church definitely provided the structure and well-defined rules for living, which provided a great comfort to her.

In the summer when I was eleven, I rode my bicycle to the community pool in the morning and spent the entire day swimming. Those were wonderful days of making friends, playing water games, and learning new tricks off the diving board. I usually returned home famished. One night we had Kentucky Fried Chicken™ for dinner, which was such a treat in those days. I must have eaten too much because I woke up during the night and barely made it to the bathroom before vomiting. I didn't wake my mother. I just flushed and went back to bed. On the second trip, I didn't quite make it to the bathroom before I threw up. My Mom awoke and lovingly cleaned up my mess. As she was putting me back to bed, she asked me why I hadn't called her. I didn't know why, but somewhere along the way I had become extremely independent. I believe it was because there were times when I *was* on my own and knew I had to take care of situations myself. More likely, it was my perception that my role was to take care of myself so that Mom wouldn't leave.

It was 1974. I was barely thirteen and had just begun to make a few close friends when we moved from a small town in Texas to the big city of Nashville, Tennessee—a big city to me anyway. We might as well have moved to the moon. We were far, far away from all our family, friends and anything familiar. I don't believe Mom's intention was to ruin my life as a teenager, but it felt that way at the time. My parents had divorced the previous year and my mother remarried a man who grew up in Nashville. He lost his job shortly after they married and he believed that employment opportunities would be much better in Nashville than in our small rural town. We moved into the house in which he was raised.

So many things were different. I went from private school to public school, from one classroom to many classrooms (I stayed lost most of the first six weeks), and from a racially segregated school to a fully integrated school. I loved to play basketball, so I was thrilled to make the school basketball team. This was the 1970's and I was no fashion goddess. I was glad to be able to wear jeans and flannel shirts instead of dresses and skirts. Life in the city presented many opportunities. While I can look back and recognize these things now, at that time all I felt was pure agony, loss, and sadness. Although I didn't label it as such, that was probably my first experience with depression. My mother recalls that I cried through most of my teenage years.

Since no one talked about manic-depression when I was growing up, we had no context for understanding what my mother was going through. In fact, I never felt there was anything unusual about my mother when I was young. I don't specifically recall her having mood swings. Nevertheless, being in the presence of my bipolar mother and under the influence of her choices, I felt the subtle, albeit significant, impact of her behavior and those decisions.

I knew she liked to spend money when she had it. On the other hand, she managed money very well when she didn't have it. She attended church and read the Bible. She had friends and was close to her cousins and my father's family. She cooked our meals, made our clothes, and kept the house spotless (with some help from me). I thought she was Superwoman with endless energy, drive, and discipline.

Mom's Physical Illnesses

At some point, my mom decided she was hypoglycemic (low blood sugar) because she showed many of the symptoms. As a result, she became very disciplined about not eating refined sugar. She was a great cook and was not afraid to try new recipes, so my family experienced a diverse spectrum of foods from different cultures. Mom baked fresh whole wheat bread regularly and made sure we ate a lot of vegetables. Even as nutritionally conscientious as she was, it seemed that she constantly had severe health problems. While I now believe that her moods were cycling, she didn't exhibit the typical symptoms. Instead, they showed up as severe physical illness.

A year or so after we moved to Nashville, Mom had her gall bladder removed, and a year later, she had a full hysterectomy. After her gall bladder surgery, she would have spasms in her stomach that were excruciatingly painful. During one episode several years later, she called and asked me to take her to the emergency room because she was having one of her stomach attacks. I was studying for the CPA exam at the time, so I gathered my study materials and rushed her to the hospital. She was immediately admitted and given some powerful medication for the pain. The drugs weren't working and no one at the hospital was doing anything about it. I felt so afraid and helpless as I watched my mother crawl around on the hospital bed trying to find a comfortable position. After the pain finally subsided and she recovered, I felt guilty for being frustrated that her illness had once again caused a major disruption in my life—especially at such a critical time.

In 1985, she was diagnosed with breast cancer. In those days, the most prevalent treatment was a mastectomy (surgical removal of the breast) followed by chemotherapy and/or radiation. She was very brave as she made the decision to go forward with the mastectomy, and very fortunate that she didn't require chemotherapy or radiation. After she recovered, she went back to work for three or four years, but she might as well have undergone a lobotomy, because she was never quite the same. Perhaps because her body stopped producing the same level of natural hormones, the chemistry in her entire body (including her brain) was thrown out of balance. She began to experience more frequent and extreme mood swings.

Mom's First Crash

The first time I remember my mother really "crashing" was just before I moved to Pittsburgh. She had been in a manic (high energy) state for a very long time. She went back to college as I was finishing high school. Within three years, she had graduated cum laude with an accounting degree. It was very rare for the large accounting firms to hire anyone over 23 years old, but my mother landed a job with one of the largest firms in the world. With two children living at home and a new demanding job, she still managed to pass the CPA exam the first time she took it. At that time, only two percent of the people who took the exam passed it the first time.

Although Mom had always leaned on me for emotional support, she usually talked about her relationships or her fear of not being smart enough (go figure). She never talked about being overwhelmed or depressed. After her mastectomy, things were different. She began talking about suicide and she could barely function. By early 1988, she had sunk into a very deep depression. Her therapist referred her to reputable doctors who began treating her with a variety of drugs and other therapies. At one point, a doctor who diagnosed her with manic-depression, began treating her with lithium. Because the lithium made her sick, Mom decided the doctor had misdiagnosed her and stopped taking the lithium. She continued searching for treatments that would relieve her depression. One of those treatments was electro-convulsive therapy (ECT) or electric shock. After undergoing ECT three times in 1990, my mom lost parts of her memory and began having difficulty finishing her sentences. At times she still falters for words. She must have been in a lot of emotional pain to endure such horrendous treatments.

As a child, I had been there to care for her during recovery from many major surgeries and illnesses, but by this time, I had moved more than 600 miles away. Therefore, the impact on my life was not as great as it was for my younger brother and sister. Even with the distance separating us, I felt as though she was trying to suck me back into the parenting role that I had managed to free myself from when I moved to Pittsburgh. I simply couldn't continue to be Mom's caretaker. Fortunately, by then she was married to her third husband who was willing to take on that role. He was extremely involved in her care—attending her therapy sessions and doctor's appointments and administering her medications.

Mom's illness did have a major impact on me. To this day, I have difficulty being completely open about my feelings because I don't want to hurt anyone else. As a result, I keep my true emotions bottled inside until I over react to a seemingly small incident. Many times, I was not being honest with myself about my feelings. I spent most of my life taking care of others and paid little attention to how *I* felt. I simply adapted to those around me. As a result, I found myself in a deep, deep depression by age forty. I had lost all hope and wanted to end the pain by ending my life.

My difficulty with honestly expressing my feelings led to difficulty setting healthy boundaries. If someone invaded my space, physical or otherwise, I would not say anything for fear of hurting his or her feelings. I also found myself guessing at how someone was reacting to something I said. If I felt the slightest bit of uneasiness, I assumed I had said something wrong or offensive. If I apologized, I often got a very puzzled look because there was no reason for me to apologize.

Setting boundaries and getting my mom to respect those boundaries has been a challenge for me—even as an adult. Several years ago, Mom decided to use an online dating service. She had not told me about it, but my sister had mentioned it during one of our phone calls. Then, my mom happened to call me at work on a Friday and shared her new adventure. She told me that one of the men was coming from Atlanta to see her that weekend. There was also this other very nice man from New Jersey that she had been talking to on a regular basis. I thought nothing of it except that she was spending a lot of time away from her doctoral studies. The following Monday morning I received a phone call at the office. This very nice gentleman, who I didn't know, informed me that he was a friend of my mom's, and that he was very concerned about her. He had tried all weekend to reach her, but she had not returned any of his calls. Since she had been ill recently, he was worried that something was wrong. There were a lot of things running through my mind—I admit that my mom's health was not at the top of the list. First of all, who was this guy?! He sounded very nice and very concerned about Mom, but I had no idea who he was and how he got my phone number! Secondly, I wondered how this man my mom met on the Internet knew my name and enough about me to reach me at work. Thirdly, I wanted to know what else he knew about me! I immediately called my mom to find out what was going on. She giggled when I told her about the phone conversation and admitted that she had been busy with her visitor from Atlanta all weekend and didn't feel it was appropriate to return the other gentleman's calls. I asked why she had shared so much information about me with a total stranger. She said that he had shared information about his children, so she thought it would be okay. It never occurred to her that she might be crossing a line with her children by sharing such details. This is just one example of Mom's challenge with honoring and respecting boundaries.

I am the oldest of three children. My sister and brother were gracious enough to share their stories for this book. You will see how differently three children growing up in the same household with the same bipolar parent viewed our individual experience. As my mother's illness progressed, her behavior still had an impact on each of us. We each took our own challenges into adulthood.

My Sister's Story

Cyndie is my younger sister and her perception of Mom's diagnosis and various treatments is vastly different from mine. Her experience with our mom was quite different from mine since her illness progressed after I left home. This is her story.

I don't believe Mom is really sick. When I heard she had been diagnosed with bipolar disorder, I thought it was just another in a long line of diagnoses that she has used to excuse her actions, behavior and choices. I do recognize that she has had a rough life, especially her childhood, but I don't think Mom is different from anyone else. After all, each of us has our own challenges to face as adults.

There have been many times in my own life when I could have admitted myself to the hospital or a treatment program in order to avoid the responsibilities of my life, but I didn't. I sucked it up, tried harder, and made it through. Mom can accomplish what she wants to, when she wants to. She is smart and so creative. She seems to have a selective illness that only comes into play when life gets too hard or when she loses interest.

Mom and I clashed a lot when I was a teenager. She was inconsistent with discipline and sent mixed messages about her expectations. I was the rebellious child, but I didn't see Mom as a parent. She seemed very focused on her own needs and not the needs of her children. This first became apparent to me in junior high school when she moved to an on-campus apartment to finish college and left my brother and me alone to live with our abusive step-father.

I often wondered if Mom loved me. She wasn't there to support me emotionally, yet I was expected to keep house, do the grocery shopping, and make meals once my older sister left for college. Life was usually about Mom's needs, which left my brother, David, and me to fend for ourselves.

When I was in high school, I was involved in a car accident

and was taken to the emergency room. A nurse phoned Mom to get permission to treat me. Mom never came to the hospital to make sure I was okay or to take me home, so I called my boyfriend for a ride. He took me to his house because I had a concussion and was not supposed to be left alone. When I did come home early in the evening, I remember Mom's first question being, "Why didn't you clean the kitchen before you left?"

When I was fifteen, Mom grounded me for some misbehavior, but since she wasn't home to enforce it, I went to a friend's apartment where some older guys lived. When I got home that evening, Mom had locked the doors and told me that I had been kicked out of the house. I was barefoot, wearing only a pair of shorts and a shirt. I had no personal items so I went back to my friend's apartment. I was mad and scared at the same time. She made it clear that I was not allowed to come back. But, after a week, she suddenly told me that I had better get home before she called the cops to tell them I had run away. Life was full of these inconsistencies and mixed messages.

I lost respect for my mom at an early age because of the decisions she made. Mom stayed with her second husband long after she knew what a monster he was. Early in their relationship, he had expressed a desire to send all of us away to boarding school. At one point I remember him threatening to kill us all in our sleep so Mom had all the guns removed from the house. I can remember Mom telling me not to let him see me cry because that's what he wanted.

Mom also allowed her third husband to completely control her life and her treatments. He would read about an illness, and then convince her psychiatrist that she had that disease. As a result, Mom endured electric shock treatments, tried different medications, and received countless diagnoses during their eight-year marriage.

Being raised by my mother created several challenges for me as an adult. I have difficulty voicing my needs in adult relationships, and I put everyone else's wants before my own. If I personally want or need something, I take care of it myself.

I'm a very independent person, and that's good—except that I have difficulty knowing how to truly open my heart and be vulnerable with someone. I have utilized counseling and other avenues to overcome or improve in these areas but still struggle with them.

Inner strength is very important to me and, as a result, I am very hard on myself when it comes to being weak. My mother was once a very strong-willed person but I watched that trait dissolve over the years. Now I see her as weak and needy, unable to take care of herself as she once did. She used to preach, "Get an education, and make your own living. Don't depend on a man!" Yet, Mom has been dependent on someone else most of her adult life.

When I'm sick, I hate to take medicine. I believe this comes from all the years I watched Mom go to doctors who diagnosed her with different illnesses (both physical and mental). Each new diagnosis came with its own set of medications she had to take. Sometimes it is very hard for me to be around her because she takes so many different medications. Sometimes she shakes and she has a hard time finishing her sentences. I feel sad that she isn't able to have an active, productive life.

I get very frustrated with those who could help themselves but choose to depend on someone else to give them what they want. For that reason, I have set very clear boundaries with my mom and she understands not to cross them.

As adults, we build on what we learned as children. I don't blame Mom for any of my own difficulties as an adult. Thanks to my life experiences, I know who I am and what I want in life. I admit that my view of Mom's diagnosis may be limited, and there is a possibility that she is suffering from bipolar disorder. My view comes from the many times in the past when I believed her diagnosis only to be told, "Oh, that's not it after all."

I want what's best for my mom but I have learned over the years to keep a little bit of distance. I am here if she needs me, but I also have my life and priorities with my own children. At least I know what *not* to do as a parent from the example that she gave me. My children have not gone a day in their lives without hearing and seeing how much I love them. They know that I value their feelings and that they are very important to me.

My attitude and opinions should not lead one to believe that I do not love my mother—quite the contrary. I love her very much and we still talk and interact frequently. Bipolar or not, my mother is who she is and I am now comfortable with the relationship that we have.

My Brother's Story

My brother, David, is eight years younger than I am and he is the youngest in our family. David believes that Mom's recent diagnosis and her current treatments are having a positive effect on her. Here is my brother's story in his own words.

The general description of our family life was mere craziness. It was one thing after another—my mom's health problems, her temper tantrums, her bad choices, and her inability to get along with people. Outsiders usually see the big picture easier than those immersed in a situation, but even as a young boy I knew that Mom's behavior wasn't right. Life wasn't supposed to be that chaotic!

The relationships Mom had with men were always negative. She married her second husband when I was four. I never did like him. Their fights were loud and emotional. Even though they fought behind closed doors, I could hear loud booms and bangs. I figured Mom had the edge, so I didn't feel the need to rescue her. I just stayed out of the way. They separated by the time I was in seventh grade.

Mom is a very intelligent woman—always a perfectionist who carries things to the maximum. If it was Thanksgiving dinner, we had to have all the trimmings. At Christmas, every decoration was picture-perfect and even the wrapping paper matched the tree. Mom had the best of everything—her wardrobe, her home décor—it was all perfect no matter how much she had to go into debt. When she went to college, she had to be the "straight A" student even if it meant neglecting her family.

I was twelve when Mom left me with my step-father, to go live on campus and finish college. My needs were not important to her. I had to remind her several times to take me to get school supplies, new clothes, or shoes. I did my own cooking and laundry. I had no accountability or supervision because when my step-father was around, he didn't care what I did as long as I stayed out of his way. There was no one to guide me or make sure I had finished my homework, so I became my own parent. I even forged Mom's name on my report card. As a latch key kid, if I misplaced my key, I would be locked out of the house until eight or nine o'clock on a school night while waiting for somebody to get home. I felt totally abandoned by my mother.

In ninth grade, I was on the wrestling team, and Mom didn't come to any of my matches. When I made the tournament finals and came home to tell her, she said, "Oh, I didn't know you were that good!" The summer I turned sixteen, I made it all the way to the Junior Olympics as a decathlete, but she still didn't go to any of my meets. My coach was my only moral support. During the last competition, I was getting ready to pole vault when my coach walked over and said, "Your mom is here." I had to make the Olympics before she came to watch me! That reinforced in me the belief that I had to do big things in order to get her attention or be seen as valuable.

I believe her high expectations of me created issues for me as an adult. I also chose accounting as my career—as Mom had. But, I wasn't satisfied to just work in public accounting—for a small firm. No, I had to work for a big five accounting firm as my mother had. I had to be a partner in the firm and work long hours because I defined who I was by what I did and how well I did it. I believed that the only way someone would love or value me was if I did big things. I felt that my best was not good enough. I know that I am harder on myself than anybody else is. I am working to change, but I still feel inferior if I'm not perfect. I am a perfectionist like my mom.

Because of my childhood experience with Mom, I practice an opposite style of parenting. I make sure I spend time with my kids. My sons are very involved in various sports. I attend every practice and every game. It doesn't matter how good they are, I am there to support them. I hated having to get up on my own, make my own breakfast, get to the bus stop, and find a way to get home from a sports event. My kids don't ride the bus. I get up every morning and take them to school and my wife picks them up. When I was a child, I waited too many times in the dark on the steps at school for a ride home. My kids will never have to worry about whether someone is coming to pick them up. I am completely involved in their lives and their needs come first. They know I love them and I am here for them every day.

I can tell when I talk to Mom if she is high or low. When she is depressed I don't hear from her, but when she is manic she talks a lot. The last time she visited my family and me, I could tell she was struggling with her medications or depression because she was really dragging. She could hardly carry on a conversation. I think she was dealing with some new drugs or different dosages.

Once I understood the symptoms of bipolar disorder and the highs and lows that go along with it, I was able to forgive Mom. Many times it seemed like Mom's illness was just an excuse. There are certain things that I can't excuse about her behavior, but I just make the best of whatever impact it had on me. I'm now dealing with the way I feel about myself. By simply learning more about Mom's illness and taking a look at the impact it had on me, I have been able to improve the important relationships in my life—especially the relationship with myself.

Chapter 2

Mom's Story

My mom, Wanaa, is a vivacious woman. Upon meeting her, one would never guess that she is bipolar or has had so much trauma in her life. Her father, Richard, was a gentleman in every way. He was a World War II veteran and an expert mechanic. He was handsome, quiet, and calm. Her mother, Doris, was likeable, but she had a volatile temper. She was the kind of woman people noticed when she walked into a room. She was tall with dark brown hair, high cheekbones, and an engaging smile. Although she was beautiful, it was her energy that caused one to pay attention. She had that movie star presence and confidence. Richard and Doris made a very attractive couple. Their relationship was filled with the passion and explosiveness that accompanies loving someone who has bipolar disorder.

These are my mother's memories of growing up with an undiagnosed bipolar mother.

Mother had a wild temper. When she was out of control, she physically and emotionally abused my younger sister and me. There were times when Mother would go out for the evening after locking us in a dark room until she returned home.

Mother was notorious for degrading my father, and publicly accusing him of having affairs when, in fact, she was the promiscuous one. Consequently, they argued a great deal.

During those heated disputes, I was sent to my room. I would lay awake all night listening, not knowing what might happen next.

I felt like my mother sabotaged any attempts I made to have a close relationship with my sister, father, or his family. She would tell us lies and pit us against one another. If I spoke fondly of my father, Mother was quick to tell me what a bad person he was and why I shouldn't love him.

School was a salvation for me. I learned that making good grades made my mother very happy. She would lavish me with praise, so I worked very hard to bring home straight A's and scholastic awards.

When Mother was feeling well, she would make clothes for all the children in the neighborhood. My sister and I would have beautiful, clean clothes to wear. When she was having a "spell," she stayed in bed for days and neglected us; often sending us to school dirty and hungry. Once, Mother had a prolonged episode of depression, and was unable to care for us. My sister and I were hungry so I called my grandmother to come help us. She brought food over and cared for my sister and me. After Grandma left, there was hell to pay—Mother beat me for sharing her secret. From that incident, I learned it was not acceptable to talk about what went on at home. I avoided conflict and never asked for help even if it meant going hungry. I was careful to stuff my feelings, not voice my needs, and anticipate her moods to avoid triggering my mother's rage.

In her early forties, Mother became so depressed that she shot herself in the chest. Although she sought treatment for her depression, the doctors knew very little about mental illness in those days. So she was treated with Valium and sent on her way.

It took many years of therapy for me to feel safe enough to recall my childhood. The stress of those experiences had a significant impact on me. To this day, I have a strong need to please others and not have anyone upset with me. I have lived a performance-based life that has driven me to exhaustion many times. I also have a great fear of abandonment. I have trouble setting boundaries and still have difficulty expressing my anger even when I need to. I experience many of the classic symptoms of bipolar disorder. At times I feel as though the cells in my body are about to explode.

I have been hospitalized at least a dozen times and have experienced paranoia, hallucinations, severe depression, manic episodes, sleep disorder, confusion, suicide attempts, post-traumatic stress disorder (PTSD), dissociative disorder, memory loss and an overall inability to handle change or stress. Throughout my life, my untreated bipolar disorder caused difficulties with my relationships, career, finances, and physical health. I have been married and divorced three times.

Because my life has been performance-based, feelings of failure are very difficult for me. I am ashamed to say that I have been fired from three jobs. The first incident occurred during a severe depression. I was working for a local accounting firm that tolerated no less than consistent peak performance. I became withdrawn as a result of my depression and was not able to complete tasks on time. As a result, I was asked to leave the firm. The second firing occurred while I was traveling to Houston on a regular basis to care for my mother who was dying from cancer. Because I was upset about the prospect of losing my mother, I shut down emotionally. This caused my performance to drop dramatically. I was working on my doctorate in accounting at the time so I could teach at the university level—a long time dream of mine. The school dismissed me from the program due to my performance. The third job loss occurred just after I had moved to the Newark, New Jersey area. I had just gotten a great job, but had difficulty finding my way around the city. I was fired because I arrived late four consecutive days as a result of getting lost.

I love to shop, and I have enjoyed many spending sprees (thanks to catalogue shopping and the QVC network). I have a passion for nice clothes and shoes. Before understanding the symptoms of bipolar disorder, I believed this passion stemmed from going without new clothes and wearing shoes with holes in them as a child. Whenever I was feeling good (manic), I would find a new hobby such as painting sweat shirts or making wreaths. Where most people would purchase materials for one or two projects, I bought enough for five or six projects. Unfortunately, when the depression set in, these projects would sit on the floor unfinished and finally be packed away. I did file bankruptcy once because I simply could not find my way out of the deep cavern of debt I created during my manic times.

I do have a mischievous side. During the years I was searching for the right treatment, I was a frequent patient at a local mental hospital. The hospital was very careful about securing the premises in order to keep patients from disappearing. Just to see if I could do it, I managed to slip out of the hospital unnoticed. Of course, my husband made me go back as soon as I called him, but it was fun to prove that I could get out if I wanted to.

Although I have no memory of it, my youngest daughter told me about a time I gave her and my granddaughter "going away" gifts. Apparently, I had planned to murder her abusive husband and then commit suicide. Fortunately, I didn't carry through with the plan—probably because I forgot about it before I did anything drastic. My daughter did say that they enjoyed their gifts.

I really didn't want people to think I was crazy, but there were times when I felt I was losing my mind. I began seeking help in the early 1980's by attending 12-step programs and codependency support groups to resolve issues resulting from my childhood. While in my early 40's I was diagnosed with depression and started taking an anti-depressant. Six months later my doctor told me I was manic-depressive and he started me on lithium along with a sleeping medication. I refused to believe that I had a mental illness. Because the lithium made me physically sick, I was convinced that the doctor had misdiagnosed me and I stopped taking it. I blamed external circumstances for my episodes. My manic phases were not typical. I don't recall having temper tantrums like my mother, nor did I get overly "happy" or euphoric. I didn't go into crazed states of risk-taking or promiscuity. Instead, I went into overdrive and became a workaholic; pushing myself to accomplish more and perform better. Sometimes my projects started small. For example, I started taking a few accounting courses and didn't stop until I had an accounting degree and CPA certificate. I worked part-time as a bookkeeper while caring for my two youngest children. I was thrilled when a large CPA firm offered me a job. It was more than I had ever dreamed of.

When I was almost 50 years old, I started walking laps around a local high school track to lose weight. I decided the pounds would fall off faster if I ran, so I began running. The next thing I knew I was training for a marathon! Of course, then I needed a new wardrobe complete with name brand running shoes, designer sunglasses, and runner's shorts. I completed the marathon twelve days before my fiftieth birthday.

In 1985, my life was turned upside down—again. On the outside I appeared to be fine, but on the inside, the physical exertion resulting from my manic bursts was taking its toll. As a result of working so hard, I bottomed out with chronic fatigue syndrome, anemia, gallbladder disease, and breast cancer.

In 2001, I stopped taking all of my medications. I was convinced that my physician, my therapist, and my boyfriend were slipping me illegal drugs. Once I was off the medications, I started hallucinating. I was unable to sleep because I just knew that someone was watching my apartment and was going to harm me. By this time, everyone around me knew there was something wrong. I was unable to function. My doctor diagnosed me with bipolar disorder. I was hospitalized in a facility with other bipolar patients. As I talked with them and heard their stories, I realized that I did have symptoms of the disease. I found it a relief to learn that other people were having similar experiences. I was able to relate to them, receive consolation, share my stories, find resources for coping, accept treatment, and finally begin to understand the mystery of my condition.

I realized that bipolar disorder was part of my life whether I liked it or not. I couldn't live in denial any longer. I became more aware of my highs and lows and started tracking them. I educated myself about what I could do to help myself. As a result, I became accountable for my actions and took my medications consistently.

I believe I could have had a better childhood if my mother had been treated for manic-depression. If she had been diagnosed and received lithium, her moods would have been more balanced and she would not have been so angry. Her depression would not have been so severe and she would have been able to care for her family. However, I may have been bipolar anyway because it's hereditary, but I would have had the information much earlier and may have accepted my diagnosis the first time.

I encourage anyone experiencing symptoms of bipolar disorder to talk about it with trustworthy friends, go to support groups where you can share your stories and listen to others. Most of all, I urge you to seek professional psychiatric and medical help.

It was hard for my children, and for me, to accept my illness. One of them thought that I was a hypochondriac all those years, but each of them is accepting it at his or her own pace.

Chapter 3

What is Bipolar Disorder?

Although statistics aren't my favorite way to receive information, there are a few related to bipolar disorder that can't be ignored. I was amazed to learn that at least 2.3 million people in the United States are living with the illness. Keep in mind that these figures represent only the people who have been diagnosed. So think about it, if there are more than two million people diagnosed, that means there are a lot more who have been touched by it. So what the heck is it? Are bipolar people just crazy? Do our parents behave that way because it's simply who they are? Could our parents behave better if they just tried harder? I thought so for a long time.

My mom is a brilliant, creative woman. She holds a masters degree in accounting, she is a Certified Public Accountant, and she taught accounting at a university. Amazingly, as she was achieving these things in her life, she was also struggling with debilitating cycles of mania and depression. As you know, Mom was diagnosed with bipolar disorder in the late 1980's. She rejected the idea after treatments made her ill. She spent the next twenty years taking a myriad of drugs, undergoing multiple rounds of electro-convulsive therapy (ECT or shock treatments), and checking herself in and out of mental institutions. Obviously, my mom wanted to get well, but I didn't see it that way at the time.

Looking back on those difficult years, it seemed as though my mom was a lab rat. When one treatment didn't work there was another experiment waiting for her. I couldn't understand why she voluntarily endured all those horrible treatments. Now I realize that she was so desperate to find some relief from the daily torment of her illness that she willingly subjected herself to whatever her doctors suggested. After enduring years of ineffective treatment, my mom was again diagnosed with bipolar disorder at the age of fifty-nine. This time she accepted the diagnosis and began to respond to the treatments. While my mother's case is unusual, the amount of time required for a doctor to diagnose a bipolar case is an average of eight years from a person's first severe depression. Why is it so difficult to diagnose this illness? Why do people have to suffer for so long before receiving the correct treatments? As I researched and learned more about bipolar disorder, I began to understand the answers to these questions.

I ask that you bear with me while I "go clinical" here. In order to better understand your parent and their behavior, it's important that you have information about their illness.

According to the National Alliance for the Mentally Ill, bipolar disorder, or manic-depressive illness, is a serious brain disorder caused by a chemical imbalance and marked by wild, cyclical mood swings, which often disrupt work, school, family, and social life. The symptoms typically begin in a person's late teens or twenties and affect men and women equally. If left untreated, it can lead to suicide. The illness is often misunderstood and difficult to diagnose because its symptoms come and go in cycles that may not reappear for as much as a year.

Bipolar disorder is diagnosed at two levels of intensity—bipolar I (more severe) and bipolar II. People diagnosed with bipolar I (BPI) typically have a history of major depression and then experience at least one manic episode. For someone with untreated BPI, their mania may culminate in frenzied psychotic episodes including delusions, paranoia, and hallucinations. Many BPI patients see or hear things that do not exist or believe they have superhuman powers. The extreme highs will then be followed by deep, crippling depressions. If a person experiences an episode (mania or depression) before the age of 30, psychosis will tend to be more common and symptoms may linger between episodes. Some people with BPI will be symptom free for months or even years between episodes.

Bipolar II disorder (BPII) is characterized by major depression and a milder form of mania called hypomania. Someone who experiences hypomanic episodes may become more productive or very goal driven, but these shifts normally do not impair their ability to function. Hypomania is not accompanied by psychotic symptoms.

Let's discuss the manic phase in more detail. As a person's mood begins to shift into "manic-drive" their thoughts flow faster. For most people, their senses become keener. They see more beauty around them, food tastes better, and sex is more intense. They may literally smell a flower from yards away. They hear the notes instead of the music. Their confidence soars and they feel they can do anything. It's like electricity is pulsing through their entire body to every nerve ending. As my mom said, sometimes she feels like every cell in her body is going to explode.

Imagine an experience you have had that brought a huge thrill to you. Now, multiply that feeling by one hundred. That is what it feels like to be manic. Who wouldn't want that feeling?! On the other hand, a manic cycle may make a person irritable and quick-tempered. They don't need sleep and they may forget to eat for days. Their fast flowing thoughts and high energy may cause them to behave impulsively. They may set out on shopping sprees and spend money they don't have because they are still digging out of the hole they created during their last manic episode. Because of a heightened sex drive, they may seek out sexual encounters and take risks that could put them in harm's way. They might begin planning and making commitments for projects they will likely not be able to finish. Unfortunately, at some point they will crash and all those wonderful thoughts, ideas and big plans will vanish.

Depression is the dark side of bipolar disorder. It is the

black abyss of intense fear, deep sadness, and lack of interest in anything. A person who is depressed may sleep for days or sit in a chair staring into space. During depressed cycles, one's thoughts are like molasses and it's difficult to concentrate. That's why they're unable to finish those projects they started while they were manic. They simply can't think clearly enough to function. They also don't have the energy to function. The simple task of getting out of bed becomes huge. They lose all hope that they will ever feel better and all they want to do is end the pain any way possible. Hopefully, they will make it to the doctor before doing harm to themselves.

There are times when a bipolar person experiences a balancing out of their brain chemicals. These phases are called euthymia (you-THIMM-ee-uh). Additionally, there are "mixed moods" where the person is both depressed and manic simultaneously. The periods of high and low mood swings do not follow a set pattern in all bipolar patients. A person may experience the same mood several times before experiencing its opposite. Are you beginning to understand why it's so difficult to diagnose bipolar disorder?

My mom's doctor, Daniel L. Friedman, M.D., was kind enough to talk with me about Mom's case and bipolar disorder in general. Dr. Friedman is a clinical psychiatrist who received his medical degree and a PhD in pharmacology from Case Western University. He conducted his residency at Vanderbilt University. He has been working with my mom since 1998. Dr. Friedman told me that patients were typically treated for symptoms of depression first—years before bipolar disorder was diagnosed. People usually seek treatment when they feel bad (depressed), not when they feel fantastic as most people do when they're manic. A patient will seek professional help after they crash and are unable to function due to depression. Because there are no blood tests or brain scans to detect bipolar disorder, doctors must base their diagnosis on information they gather from the patient.

I don't know about you, but I have rarely spent more than twenty minutes with any medical professional. They typically draw their conclusions and reach a diagnosis based on information I provide them about how I'm feeling—either physically or emotionally. Since the more conclusive forms of testing like brain scans are not yet available, how would a doctor know if someone is bipolar? Unless the patient is aware enough to explain to the physician that they are manic or unless someone else who knows them shares this information, it is unlikely that the doctor will witness the manic symptoms. I'm not saying that all doctors are morons about detecting the disorder. If the doctor is well trained, he or she will know to ask probing questions about family history and to watch for patterns in a patient's behavior. However, based on what I have read, heard, and experienced, the symptoms that would lead to an accurate diagnosis will likely go unnoticed for a long time if the only opportunity to observe a patient's behavior is a series of short visits.

If an accurate diagnosis by a trained professional is difficult for people looking for help, just imagine how difficult it is for those who live with the hellish symptoms without knowing anything about the condition. For instance, Julie Fast, author of "Loving Someone with Bipolar Disorder," wrote "I finally realized that all the sounds I heard in my head weren't normal. I realized that seeing myself get killed by a car, mauled by a dog or smashed by a truck wasn't normal. I realized that the voices I thought were my own negative thoughts were actually hallucinations." For the millions of people who have sought help, many more have struggled with their mood swings and other symptoms not knowing that relief was available. Unfortunately, as they struggled to deal with their condition, their loved ones grappled with the fall-out.

Because bipolar disorder is diagnosed by noting the severity, frequency, and duration of symptoms, it may be necessary for the doctor to collect information from family members. While it is not your responsibility to diagnose your parent, you can significantly enhance your relationship with them by becoming aware of what bipolar disorder looks like. If they are showing signs of this illness, please seek the help of a trusted doctor.

Instead of being frustrated by your parent's behavior, you can watch for shifts in their emotions and take the necessary action to help your parent manage through their mood swing until they stabilize. If your parent chooses not to seek treatment, your knowledge and awareness of the symptoms will go a long way in helping you maintain a healthier relationship with your parent. It's a tough disease and those who suffer with it know when they have alienated their family and friends. This awareness may intensify their irritation (and downward spiral if they are depressed) because they feel guilty.

Symptoms

It may be helpful for you to have a quick list of symptoms. This list is not all inclusive since bipolar is very complex and shows up differently for each person. However, it will help you understand behaviors that many bipolar people exhibit. The following list was taken from the *DBSA Manual Finding Peace of Mind*. You may use them as a checklist to monitor your parent's condition.

A depressive episode will usually last at least two weeks and will be accompanied by at least five of the following symptoms:

_____ Sadness and crying spells for no reason

_____ Major changes in appetite and sleep patterns

_____ Irritability and anger

_____ Worry and anxiety

_____ Pessimism, indifference, and/or feelings that nothing will ever go right

_____ Loss of energy and/or constant exhaustion

_____ Unexplained aches and pains

_____ Feelings of guilt, worthlessness, and/or hopelessness

_____ Inability to concentrate or make decisions

_____ Loss of interest in things once enjoyed

_____ Reluctance to socialize or to talk to others

_____ Excessive alcohol or drug use

_____ Recurring thoughts of death or suicide

_____ Difficulty facing day-to-day challenges or mundane tasks like driving a car or going to work or school

_____ Withdrawal from social situations

A manic episode will be accompanied by at least three of the following symptoms:

_____ Increased physical and mental activity

_____ Extreme optimism and self-confidence or feeling anything can be accomplished no matter how difficult the task

_____ Grandiose thoughts and feelings of increased self-importance

_____ Irritable, agitated, angry, nervous, "on edge" or "out of sorts" for no reason

_____ Easily distracted

_____ Aggressive behavior that may include violence

_____ Decreased need for sleep without feeling tired

_____ Racing speech and/or thoughts along with
        excessive talking
_____ Impulsiveness, poor judgement
_____ Reckless behavior such as spending sprees, major
        business decisions, careless driving and sexual
        promiscuity
_____ Delusions and hallucinations (seeing or hearing
        things that don't exist)
_____ Paranoia (someone or something is lurking)

There are other symptoms that practitioners look for as well. A predisposition for alcohol and drug abuse is caused by a chemical imbalance. Approximately 60 percent of individuals with bipolar disorder also have drug abuse or alcohol dependence and 70 percent of those in alcohol and drug abuse treatment programs also have mental illness. When a person demonstrates two forms of mental illness, it's referred to as dual diagnosis. Until recently, the two were treated separately. The best recovery program for those with bipolar disorder and drug/alcohol abuse diagnoses is Dual Recovery Anonymous (DRA), which uses an integrated approach to address both mental illness and drug or alcohol abuse simultaneously with medication, psychotherapy, and support groups. Refer to Appendix A for resources that provide more information about DRA.

While bipolar disorder occurs equally in women and men, women tend to experience more periods of depression and switch moods more often than men. Frequent shifts in mood are referred to as "rapid cycling" and may be due to activity of the thyroid gland. The mental health profession defines a person as "rapid cycling" if they experience four or more mood swings within a 12-month period.

Possible Causes

The three known causes or triggers of bipolar disorder are heredity, stress, and brain chemistry imbalance. Since the illness is still being studied, there may be other causes. What scientists do know is that it tends to run in families. Stress can trigger it or make it worse. Medications that help correct levels of mood regulating chemicals in the brain also relieve the symptoms. We will briefly look at each of these causes separately.

Heredity

Research seems to indicate that many people are born with a predisposition to mental illness. Among all mental illnesses, bipolar disorder may have the greatest genetic involvement. Relatives of people suffering from bipolar illness are 10 to 20 times more likely to develop the condition than the general population. From the data gathered in family, twin, and adoption studies, it is evident that genetic factors are involved in the transmission of the disease. Scientists are searching for the genes and the brain proteins that account for vulnerability to bipolar disorder.

Before you freak out and throw this book across the room because scientific data suggests that you might be bipolar by default, remember that this disorder is far from consistent. Although my mother is bipolar, none of her children have been diagnosed and we're all adults so it should have shown up by now! More than half the people interviewed for this book were not diagnosed as bipolar even though their parents were. I am simply presenting research results for information purposes. Don't despair. Just stay with me and learn more so that you can take care of yourself or a loved one who begins to show signs of mania or depression.

Stress

Environmental factors and major life changes such as a loss of a job, the birth of a child, a death in the family or relocating the household seem to trigger the onset of symptoms in bipolar disorder. Once the symptoms begin, they will usually progress and continue to cycle. Any condition that emotionally upsets a person may possibly set off an episode of depression or mania.

Brain Chemical Levels

Although scientists have identified a strong tie, the link between BPI and DNA is not yet clear. According to studies published by the American Journal of Psychiatry and the University of Michigan, the brain of a bipolar person is "wired" differently than a non-bipolar person. There is a neuro-chemical difference between bipolar patients and non-bipolar people. The studies indicated that, for the bipolar participants, two major areas of the brain (the thalamus and the ventral brain stem) contained thirty percent more cells that send signals to other brain cells (neurons). This results in over-stimulation for people who have bipolar disorder. Using a brain imaging technique called positron emission tomography (PET), researchers have been able to see the density of cells that release the brain chemicals dopamine, serotonin and norepinephrine. These chemicals (monoamines) are involved in mood regulation, stress responses, and cognitive functions like concentration, attention, and executive functions. PET scans show that there is a difference in the density of chemical-releasing cells in the brains of bipolar people even when they are not experiencing symptoms. The more monoamine cells a patient had, the lower their scores were on tests of executive function and verbal learning which are known to affect cognitive and social function. Further studies hope to discover both genetic and chemical components and their exact roles in mental illness.

I stayed angry with my mom for many years. I didn't trust her and felt as though she tried to manipulate me. Moving 600 miles away didn't resolve any of my issues with her behavior—it just delayed my dealing with them. I felt that she lied to me and stepped over the boundaries I set with her. As a result, we didn't have any real mother/ daughter conversations for a long time. During those years, I didn't rely on her for emotional support. I felt as though our roles were reversed. As I have become more aware of her illness and understand that it results from an imbalance in her brain chemistry, I can deal with her behavior. Now I'm more supportive and patient with her. She has also done very well by sticking with her treatment program that includes medications and talk therapy. With a lot of hard work, she's now more stable.

In the next section you will meet four very courageous, incredible survivors. Their stories are horrifying and inspiring. I have included them because they provide different perspectives on whether it is healthy to maintain a relationship with a bipolar parent. Note that aliases have been used to protect those interviewed and their families.

PART TWO

DETOURS & DERAILMENTS

Chapter 4

Life on Red Alert

R ed alert!" she shouted as she hung up the telephone. Everyone knew what she meant and they dreaded the outcome. Over the next two weeks, Mona Avery's household would be turned upside down and inside out. Her six children would scrub the floors, polish the furniture, wash baseboards, paint their bedrooms, and whatever she felt needed to be done to make the house spotless. She would carefully check each part of every project to make sure it was performed to her high standards. Sometimes she would purchase new bed linens or drapes during a Red Alert—just because. Family would be visiting soon and everything had to be perfect.

Mona Avery's father was a Baptist preacher on Sundays and a bootlegger the rest of the week. He abused his wife and children physically, sexually, spiritually, and emotionally. Mona was the oldest of seven children and she took the brunt of the beatings in order to protect her younger siblings. Her father used a razor strap to discipline his family. If Mona's mother heard the family car screeching toward the house, she would hurry the children and dogs to the barn where they would stay until he had time to cool down.

Clearly, Mona's father had a deadly temper. One of Mona's children shared, "My grandfather was not only mentally ill, he had demons inside, which he was trying to rectify or balance with religion." Although he was never diagnosed with a mental illness, his mother was diagnosed with manic depressive disorder.

Mona was just fourteen when she married the high school quarterback, who was four years older. They were both products of very abusive childhoods. He had endured years of physical and sexual abuse. By the time she was twenty-one, Mona had given birth to five children—two girls and three boys. She went to the doctor to seek help for her nerves. He prescribed Valium and suggested that she continue taking it until her children were grown. Little did he know that Mona was dealing with far more than her children.

The only two emotions that Mona ever showed were fear and anger. Her anger was deadly like her father's. Although she didn't use a razor strap, she would throw or beat her children with whatever household item was handy—a coat hanger, soupspoon, or spatula.

Mona was obsessed with cleaning her house. Over several days, she would pull everything out and scour the rooms. Of course, she would completely exhaust her energy, so the children were left to put everything back in its place. Whenever she painted the interior walls, she used white paint because white was clean. Mona's mother was also a clean fanatic. If you weren't clean, you were considered "white trash." Mona learned this philosophy at a very young age and passed it on to her own children. Later in her life she confided in one of her daughters, "You know, I think I've about killed myself all these years trying not to be 'white trash' and trying to please my dead mother!"

On two occasions, Mona attempted suicide. The first time occurred when she learned about her husband's affair. She was in her early thirties and was terribly distraught. She tried again less than ten years later. During this time there was never a confirmed diagnosis of bipolar disorder. Mona continues to take only the Valium. As she grows older, her children have noticed that her mood swings have begun to occur more often and have become more pronounced.

Three of Mona's children were kind enough to share their stories and the issues born out of their difficult childhoods.

Loretta

Loretta is Mona's oldest daughter. Because there were so many children born so close together, Mona looked to her oldest daughter to assume a lot of responsibility at a tender age. This is her story.

Because of the chaos in our house and my mother's rages, I learned very early in life how to size up a situation and the energy involved. I took whatever measures necessary to keep bad things from happening. I was very much a peacemaker and took on the role of protector.

I remember standing on a chair at the age of five or six—ironing clothes or hanging them out to dry. I was overwhelmed with responsibility and felt a tremendous amount of anxiety. In some respects, I became the parent because my parents were so young and didn't know what they were doing.

When I was in second grade, I dropped a glass jar in the kitchen and broke it. My mother slapped me so hard that I fell on the broken glass and cut a gash in my knee. To stop the bleeding, she took a handful of flour and put it in the gash. I still have a bad scar and probably should have been taken to the emergency room for stitches, but Mother just went on about her business in the kitchen.

One day, when I was in third grade, I missed the school bus. We hopped in the car to see if we could catch the bus. We lived in a rural area, so school was not close. We located the bus moving slowly down the road. Mother started honking the horn, but the bus driver didn't pull over. The whole event turned out to be quite a pursuit with Mother raging and honking the horn. Suddenly, the hood of the car flew up. This must have fueled my mother's fury because I checked out after that and I don't remember how the episode ended. This is just one memory I have of my mother exhibiting extreme reactions to ordinary situations. Her responses were confusing and scary to me as a child, but they also provided some perspective later when I began to understand her illness.

Because our family moved a lot, I attended ten schools in three different states. Shortly after I left home to attend college, my family moved three hours away from where we had been living. No one called to let me know they were moving or where they were going. I tried calling home and, of course, the number had been disconnected. For two weeks, I couldn't find my family. I remember sitting in my dorm room and crying because I felt totally abandoned. Mother felt that, since I was off at college having a good time, I was taken care of. She had five other children to worry about and it simply didn't occur to her to call me. She gave no thought to the impact that her lack of communication would have on me.

In my extended family, there was a man we called Grandpa Nash who had molested me when I was a child. When I was twenty-three years old, I attended a family reunion and Grandpa Nash happened to be there. My mother knew that he had molested me, yet she made a point to take me over to him. He was in a wheel chair by this time. My mother said, "Loretta, do you remember Grandpa Nash?" I felt totally victimized. The look in Mother's eyes was almost sadistic as she stood there playing this terrible game with my emotions. I will never forget that look. I thought to myself, "What the hell is going on here? Why is my mother putting me in front of this man who molested me?" I didn't know what to do other than get away from him as quickly as possible. I felt as though my horrible experience and the memory of it didn't matter to her.

Because I was a parent to my younger siblings, I didn't even know I had needs, much less have a chance to voice them or get them met. Even though there was food on the table and a roof over my head, I was so busy taking care of my mother and siblings that there was no time to think about anything else.

I never had any privacy when my mother was around. Even after I become an adult, she felt comfortable opening and looking at all of my mail. Clearly, I had no privacy and there were no boundaries where my mother was concerned.

The defining moment for me occurred just before I turned forty. Mother and I had a conversation and I felt we were on the same page by the end of it. Days later, I referred to something we had discussed and she had no recollection of the conversation. She became very uncomfortable when I told her we had talked about this particular topic. That's when I saw it—she switched personalities right in front of me! She became the out-of-control angry person I had known as a child. When I stood my ground with her, she switched into her victim personality. It was my first realization that she had a serious problem. Because I had received counseling and had done some research, this incident was less threatening to me and I was able to see it from an observer's viewpoint. I realized that it wasn't all me, that there was something strange about Mother's behavior, and that I hadn't caused it! This was my stepping off place. I could stop trying to create sanity from insanity. It was a huge relief and I was able to feel compassion for my mother. In that moment, I decided I had enough and got off the "family game board." For five years, I had no contact with my family except for my sisters. During those years, I did a lot of work on myself and developed tools for dealing with Mother. I gradually built the courage to start communicating again with her. I felt strong enough to maintain my boundaries because I had learned not to be the victim in Mother's attempts at manipulation.

Realizing that the insanity was not about me, that it was about my mother's illness, was one of the most freeing experiences in my life. The insanity was not my fault. Although it had an impact on my life, I knew for the first time that her behavior was not because of something inherently wrong with me. I breathed a sigh of relief because I could stop trying to fix everything. My decision to let go of the responsibility and the need to create sanity from insanity, allowed me to begin the journey of healing the deep wounds I had carried all my life. When I let go of my mother, the healing began for me.

Doris

Doris is Mona's third child. Her earliest memories are marked by her mother's extreme mood swings and the physical and emotional abuse that went along with them. Here is her perspective.

My mother could be a sweet and kind person one minute, and become mean and deadly in the next. When she was happy, she took us on picnics in the park or to Brownie meetings. When her anger erupted, we knew to take cover and get out of her way. Even though this was typical behavior for my mother, I knew at an early age that something wasn't right about her. My friends' mothers didn't act like that.

My mother was proud of the fact that if she called something black, we had to agree with her regardless of the color. I learned this lesson the hard way by continuing to question her. This usually resulted in me getting slapped in the face three or four times while she told me how stupid I was and that I'd better keep my mouth shut. Naturally, I grew up believing that I was very stupid and incompetent. As a young child, I remember going to the mirror after my mother hit me and saying, "I hate her! I hate her! I hate her! I will never, ever be like her!"

When I was fourteen, my brother's girlfriend wrote him a note in which she called him a "punk." At that time, the word meant "smart-mouth." My mother found the note in my brother's jeans and went absolutely ballistic. She phoned his girlfriend, called her several choice names, and told her never to set foot in our house again. We had no idea why she had been so upset about the note until many years later. We learned that the term "punk" to her generation referred to a prison inmate's sex partner. A few days after the incident, I went to the girl's house to apologize for my mother's bizarre behavior. Mother found out about it and slapped me around screaming, "When are you going to learn to keep your mouth shut? Why can't you use your head for something besides a hat rack? You are so stupid!" That was the day I stopped questioning my mother and I completely shut down.

Our parents insisted that we not discuss our private lives with others; therefore, the outside world didn't see the insanity and the abuse. My parents taught me to act like a "lady"—a dignified, sexually pure girl. At the same time, people in our immediate and extended families were sexually abusing my sisters and me. The conflicting message was confusing. When I was six years old, I mustered the courage to tell some people at our church that I was being sexually abused. They confronted my parents who, of course, lied to the church members. My mother cried because she was so embarrassed that I would say such a thing. My dad beat me silly for telling the family secret. The church members told me not to worry because God would take care of me. The abuse continued and by the time I was seven years old I felt as though God had completely abandoned me.

Even though Mother rarely worked outside the home and was physically around us, she was not emotionally available to us. I remember standing at her knee when I was very young, tugging on her apron, and trying to get her to notice me. She always seemed distracted. Once she took me with her to visit my aunt. When she left, she took off without me. I was terrified and I ran down the road screaming, "Momma! Momma! Wait! You forgot me!" She came back and was horrified that she had been so lost in her thoughts that she had forgotten me. It's a funny memory now but I'm surprised it only happened once.

I coped with her behavior by shutting down and becoming very quiet and submissive. I learned to tune out her ranting and raving. When things got too scary, I would completely dissociate from the situation.

Because Mother told me over and over that I was stupid, I had a difficult time believing in myself. For a long time, I wouldn't try anything new for fear of failure, which would only prove that she was right. I was about twenty-eight years old when I realized that my life was a total mess. Even though I didn't want to be like my mother, I became aware that I had picked up some of her negative traits. Fortunately, I recognized the patterns, apologized to my children, and began making a conscious effort to heal myself and change my behavior. I was grateful that my children were very forgiving and understanding.

When I was a child, there were no boundaries in our

household. I was thirty years old when I finally set a boundary with Mother. She had always used us to manipulate our father into doing something she wanted him to do. If we went somewhere, she could usually get Dad to go, too. On this particular occasion, she asked me to attend a church meeting so Dad would go. I said, "I already have plans tonight and I can't go." As simple as that statement sounds, it was a huge and difficult step for me. I hung up the phone and danced around my house laughing and celebrating the reality that she couldn't slap me or manipulate me anymore. It was the first step that I had to take in order for her to show me the respect that I deserved.

When she knew I wasn't home, Mother would call my children to make sure I was feeding and taking care of them. She wanted to know if I was out with a boyfriend. She would belittle me to my own children and tell them not to tell me she had called. Of course, as soon as I walked in the door, the kids would say, "Granny called." They knew from a young age that their grandmother was not emotionally stable so they told me everything she said whenever she called. I asked her to stop calling the kids while I wasn't home—she ignored me. I finally wrote her a letter telling her that as a single parent, I needed all the support I could get and that I didn't need the disrespect she was trying to foster in my children. I told her that if she couldn't change her behavior, she could stay out of our lives. I had very little contact with her for almost a year afterward. She finally understood that I meant what I said and that my boundaries were there to stay. It was a very healing experience.

The biggest lesson I learned from my own healing was the importance of forgiveness. I had to let go of my childhood abuse and release the hatred I felt toward my mother and other family members. Forgiveness is a vital part of recovery. Until I let go of my resentment, I was trapped in the past. I made the necessary changes and realized that I was capable of doing whatever I wanted with my life. Today, I am active in church and know that

God did not abandon me after all. Otherwise, I would not have lived to share my story.

Melissa

Melissa is the youngest of Mona's children. While she shares many of her sisters' childhood memories, she has some unique perceptions of her own.

❧

Memories of my mother are punctuated with her extreme mood swings. She would be bed ridden for days with depression and then would come out of it and obsessively clean the house. She never seemed to be in a good mood, and one never knew what might set her off.

With three sons and three daughters in the house, there was a lot of noise. We were always playing, screaming, talking, running through the house, or picking fights with one another. Sometimes it was more than she could handle. She would be standing at the kitchen stove stirring soup, suddenly lose her temper, and throw a spoon at one of us.

Mom had an "open door" policy for anyone in the neighborhood. There was always cake or cookies in the house or something on the stove to eat. When she wasn't depressed, she would take on multiple household projects that she had to finish all at once. She would be painting one room, stripping the floor in another, and pushing herself until she crashed and had to be in bed for days.

She was thirty-two when I was born and my older siblings say that I received the brunt of her mood swings that have continued to grow more severe and more frequent as she has gotten older. I never felt an emotional bond with my mother. Perhaps it's because she tried to kill herself when she was pregnant with my twin brother and me. My brother died as a result of her suicide attempt. In the womb, I sensed that it was not safe to form an emotional bond with the person who killed my brother. So my mother was just someone I grew up with. It's still a point of grief for me—knowing that I will never feel the unconditional love that children receive from their mothers. I don't have any memories of wanting to crawl up in my mother's lap or to have her rock me when I was sad or frightened. My older siblings fulfilled the parenting role making sure that my physical needs were met. They looked out for me as much as possible.

Because my mother and some of my siblings had abused me, I learned to dissociate. I would disappear mentally, leave my body and imagine I was a butterfly playing with the angels and the animals. After all my siblings left home and we moved to Illinois, I felt somewhat safe. At that point, I just had to deal with my mother's behavior. Believe me, that was enough!

Shortly after we moved, I went to the local swimming pool with some girlfriends. I met a boy there and spent time with him that day. When I got home, I told my mother about this nice boy. She lost it and started beating me for interacting with him! It was then that I realized there was something very wrong with my mother and it was not my fault. I knew that her extreme reactions were not normal. I experienced a shift that day which changed our relationship forever. I claimed my power and that was the last time I took a beating from my mother. Before this incident, I had been the compliant child. Afterward, I drew the line and refused to put up with her bazaar behavior.

The only thing my mother understood was extremes, so I got her attention by taking extreme action. At the age of twelve, I became very direct, cold and uncaring. I began to live my life and shut her out of it. I stayed in my bedroom most of the time because everything I wanted was there—my piano, stereo, TV, phone, and animals. I only came out to go to the bathroom or get something to eat.

When I was fourteen, the quarterback of our high school football team asked me to a dance. I shared the news with my mother who seemed to be okay with it. Later, she stormed into my bedroom yelling and screaming like a mad woman. She accused me of being promiscuous and threatened to put me on birth control pills. All this over an invitation to a dance! Much later, it occurred to me that I was the same age she was when she married my father who was also the quarterback of the football team. Who knows what triggered my mother's rage, but she always seemed to overreact.

After that incident, I began to set even more boundaries. Any time Mother tried to put me into a parenting role or asked me to do something that didn't feel right, I refused. We were constantly at war because I would not compromise my boundaries. I got to a point where I had enough and asked to go away to a boarding school. I never lived with my parents again.

With all the abuse in our family, none of us understood healthy boundaries. My mother even read my diary! What a harmful invasion of my privacy! Any parent should know that. After I became an adult, my mother continued to challenge and violate my boundaries whenever I let my guard down.

During a time when I was beginning to remember the abuse, my mother called me at work in the middle of the day. She wanted to tell me about the time she took me to the doctor and he told her that someone was sexually abusing me. I'm sure in her mind she was trying to help me, but she had absolutely no consideration for the impact the information would have on me and how I would deal with it at work. Of course, the revelation triggered a lot of painful memories that I was not prepared to handle. I wrote Mother a letter and told her that I never wanted to speak to her again. I told her how I felt about her invasion of my privacy over the years and her disregard for the boundaries that I had set.

When she got the letter, she called right away. Unfortunately, this was before caller ID so I took the phone call. I think the person who invented caller ID must have had an abusive parent! Anyway, my mother launched in, "I can't believe that you would write me this kind of letter! How could you do this to me?" During the conversation, I caught a glimpse of myself in the mirror and something sparked inside me. I said, "Don't you ever call me again! Don't you ever contact me. If you do, I will have the police after you!" I had to make it extreme in order for her to understand. She still tried to contact me, but I had decided to completely pull away from my family and unplug from the madness. I didn't speak to my parents for over five years. I didn't speak to my brothers for eight years. I had to find my sanity and work through the fall out of growing up in a household of abuse and insanity. I did stay in contact with my sisters because they had come to the same realization. We were all healing together and it was wonderful to have their support.

I am happy to say that our family dynamic is now very different. Christmas of 1997 was the first time we came together in almost ten years. Many of us had dealt with our issues. It was amazing to begin listening to their experiences and to share my own journey. I realized how connected we were. When I began to do my work and forgave certain family members, dramatic changes began to occur in their lives as well.

I am so grateful that we have been able to work through our issues. Now we can stop the patterns of abuse and the future generations will not suffer the way we did. Their relationships will be based on love instead of total dysfunction.

Chapter 5

Worst Case Scenario

Suzanne is a very intelligent woman with dark hair and sad brown eyes. You can almost feel the burden she carries. Upon meeting her, I felt compelled to take her in my arms and let her know everything would be all right. She is the youngest of three children who grew up with a bipolar mother. Here is Suzanne's story in her own words.

❧

My mother has a very good sense of humor, but her moods change like the flip of a switch. One minute she would be laughing with us and the next minute she would be hitting us with something. After I broke my ankle, I had to use crutches for a while. Mom and I were joking around and I must have made a comment she didn't like. She hit me across the back with one of the crutches.

I never knew what to expect from her. Consistency was a foreign concept in our house. We could do something one day and it would be fine, but if we did the same thing the next day, Mom would beat us. As a result, I never felt confident that what I was doing was okay.

The beatings were frequent and severe. Mother seemed to get enjoyment out of beating us. If we had not been "caught" misbehaving all week, she would beat us on Friday anyway. She hit us with whatever was in her hand.

People knew what was going on, but they didn't report it

to the authorities. You just didn't do that thirty years ago. Some people did say something to my dad about it, but nothing would ever change. The beatings were so severe that I lived in fear that my mother would kill me. One time she got mad and held a butcher knife to my throat. If Mother wasn't smiling or laughing, we couldn't smile or laugh either. If we acted too happy or if we got excited, Mother would give us one of her tranquilizers. I was small for my age and my mother was a big woman. The dosage in one of her tranquilizers would cause me to sleep for 48 hours. The beatings got progressively worse, and I was even beaten in the face.

Because she was four years older, my sister, Gina, had most of the responsibility of caring for my brother and me. She did a good job keeping us fed. At the age of nine, she did all the cooking, laundry and grocery shopping. Our mother would drop us off at the laundry mat or grocery store. When she returned, the laundry or shopping had better be done. If Gina spent more than the amount Mother allotted for groceries, there would be hell to pay. Gina used her own money to buy a plastic counting device so she would be sure she didn't buy more than allowed—anything to avoid getting beaten.

Mother never paid much attention to our hygiene. I remember neighbors saying, "Look how dirty those kids are." My brother and I would come in the house caked in mud from playing outside, and be sent to bed without a bath. We took a bath before we went to church on Sunday, but the rest of the week we were filthy.

My mom used recreational drugs on a regular basis. Many of my friends used marijuana in high school, but never offered it to me because they knew I wouldn't be interested. The only pressure I had to smoke pot was from my mother! She would shove it in my face and say, "C'mon, I know you want it. It'll mellow you out. Just smoke some. It'll be fun."

On Friday evenings, Mother would make lists of chores for each of us. Since she worked outside the home, she loved to sleep late on Saturdays. She would hand each of us a list and warn us that if we woke her, we would get a beating. If all the chores were not complete by the time she awoke, everyone would get a beating. Since we never knew what time she would wake up, we had to figure out how to vacuum without waking her.

Children should feel safe in their own home, but my siblings and I learned at a very early age that we had to be on guard with our mother at all times. We had to constantly try to outwit her. I remember a time when all three of us had recurring stomachaches and diarrhea. Because she bought all the groceries, Gina knew the frequency that Mother asked her to buy Milk of Magnesia. Our mother had been pouring full bottles of Milk of Magnesia into the gallon milk jugs from which we drank. Gina figured out what she was doing, and started marking the milk jug. If the liquid level was above the last mark, we would throw away the milk. Since we drank a lot of milk at that time, Mother didn't notice that we were pouring some of it out. When she realized that we were on to her, we got a beating, but at least she stopped putting Milk of Magnesia in our milk.

I always knew that my mother was different. Once, I saw a family photo in which I was sitting on my mother's lap. Most children in family photos sit snuggled close to their mothers. I was sitting at the end of my mother's knee as if I was ready to jump as soon as the picture was taken. I never remember feeling safe with my mother and I certainly did feel like she was ever emotionally available. When I was small, Mother hired a babysitter who was very loving and gentle with us. I felt safe with the babysitter, but not with my mother.

My mother had a terrible time with money. Even though she always worked, we lived on Dad's paycheck. No one knew what she did with her money because she never had anything to show for it. One day Dad went to get in the car and a strange man came up to him and said, "You can give me the keys, Mr. Johnson. I need to take the car because you have not paid on it for three months." Until that moment, Mother had been responsible for paying the bills. My father had set up college trust funds for all three of us, but she accessed the accounts and spent every dime.

My mother forced me to sleep with her and sexually abused me while my father was traveling on business. She continued to make inappropriate comments about my body after I was an adult. It absolutely disgusted me. I have never had success in setting boundaries with her.

We also knew that our mother was cheating on our father. She worked a night shift taking inventory for a grocery store. She had to use a ten-key calculating machine in order to do her job. There were many times she would leave without her ten-key and go the opposite direction of the grocery store when she left for "work." Finally, I saw her with another man and told my father about it. That's when dad left her. Mother became so depressed when he left that she couldn't get out of bed. She cried non-stop for three or four months. Because she wasn't able to care for us, and Gina had gone to college, my brother and I went to live with our father. At least the beatings stopped.

Mother was fired from three or four consecutive jobs after only working a couple of months. Even in those days, employers were very careful about what they put in personnel files and didn't write anything without enough evidence to defend the company in court. For one of the jobs from which she was fired, Mother's pink slip read "sexual promiscuity" which meant it must have been really bad.

My mother became psychotic when she was 53 years old and was hospitalized in 1993. She was caught walking around her apartment complex completely naked hammering twenty-dollar bills into the sides of the buildings.

The psychiatrist treating her at the time asked me, "Do you realize that your whole childhood could have been different if your mother had been diagnosed when you were young?" It was devastating to hear such a comment after surviving a nightmare childhood. He may have been right, but that certainly wasn't something I wanted to hear!

During her stay at the hospital, my mother was diagnosed bipolar with psychotic features. She began receiving treatment, and was fine for five or six years until she decided to stop taking her medicine. That's when she threw her couch over her second floor balcony onto the sidewalk, and was again caught walking naked around her apartment complex. Fortunately, the apartment manager was a friend of Gina's, or Mother would have lost her right to stay in the government-subsidized complex.

Every four or five years, Mother decides to go off her medication. Sometimes she believes her doctors are trying to poison her. Other times she doesn't think she needs the meds any longer. My mother has been in the state hospital four or five times. She continues to drink, which reduces the effectiveness of her medication. She has been drinking most of her life and has what is called "wet brain." She has killed so many brain cells that her cognitive ability is drastically diminished. She slurs her words, stops in the middle of a sentence, and searches for words to complete a thought.

Because my mother was so controlling, adult relationships have been a challenge for me. Unconsciously, I sought out people who would control me. It wasn't until I was out of the relationship that I realized how much my partners were like Mother. It has taken a long time and a lot of therapy to help me stop making those choices. There was a time when I just stopped dating. I lived alone, and worked on myself. I got my head straight before rejoining the dating scene. I have a great psychiatrist and a wonderful therapist that I've been seeing since 1993. This continuity of care makes a big difference.

Jobs have been difficult for me because of my depression. My medicine seems to stop working every so many years. I have been hospitalized five or six times since my first severe case of depression occurred in 1989. It's difficult to ferret out what exactly causes me to become depressed whether it is the medicine or something I need to work on in therapy, or a combination of the two. I'm not sure where the effects of my childhood end and the chemical imbalance I inherited begins. It would be very helpful if there was a test to determine when a chemical imbalance has occurred so we know for sure that we just need an adjustment in medication.

After years of trying to reach out to my mother for emotional support and attempting to maintain some type of relationship with her, I finally realized that to remain in contact with her would mean having to ride the constant emotional rollercoaster with her. In order to heal myself, I had to cut all ties with my mother. It was a very difficult decision because it caused a severe rift with my sister who feels that she has been abandoned to look after our mother by herself.

The last straw fell the day I learned that my brother, who always seemed to receive more emotional support from Mother, had died. In January of 2002, he passed away from an alcohol withdrawal seizure. He lived alone and the manager of his apartment complex found him several days later. The police called me to give me the news. I was very upset and called Gina. We decided that Gina would call Dad and I would call Mother. The conversation did not go well. There was a lilt in my mother's voice as she asked me how I was doing. I thought, "She doesn't know about her son yet." I reported the bad news. My mother said in the same cheery voice, "Oh, I already know." I could not fathom my mother reacting so casually to learn that her son had passed away, and said, "No, Mother, I don't think you know." She replied, "Yes, I know, your brother is gone. He has a CD player, doesn't he?" I answered hesitantly, "Yes, I believe he does have a CD player." Mom said, "Well, I have these 'Stop Smoking' CD's that I need to listen to, so I need his CD player." In the days following that conversation, I finally realized that my mother was a sociopath. I had deluded myself into believing that her behavior was due to her illness and was not part of her character. I wanted to believe that if she was properly medicated, she would be a normal person. It was then that I began having nightmares about the sexual and physical abuse of my childhood. Every time I talked to my mother, I would have more nightmares and it would take me five or six days to recover. Something had to change in order for me to remain healthy. My therapist, friends, partner, and everyone around me was saying, "Cut your mother off!" It was a resounding voice and I finally decided, eight months after my brother's death, not to have any more contact with my mother. It seems that our mother's behavior doesn't effect Gina like it effects me. She is able to put it out of her mind and not deal with it whereas it haunts me and upsets me terribly.

Because of my own experience, I would like to caution people not to blindly accept that all of their parent's behavior is due to their illness. Be careful so you won't be traumatized as an adult. I feel an affinity with my mother because we are the only two in my family who have been in a mental hospital. As a result, I believe that we understand things about one another that no one else in the family understands. There is some comfort in that.

Common Threads

As the interviews with other CBPs began to unfold, it became very clear that we had similar experiences. Our parents' behavior followed a lot of the same patterns. The next section looks at those common threads and the impact those experiences had on us. Note that the portions in *italics* represent excerpts from interviews.

PART THREE

SOJOURN SOUVENIRS

Chapter 6

Coping with Chaos

*S*omebody needs to go get that knife. Tag—you're it!" Rita said to her brother as they huddled under the bed. "Why me?" said Carl. She whispered, "You're older, and you're the boy, now go get it!" He dashed into the kitchen, grabbed the knife, and came back. As soon as he had hidden it under the bed, a second knife appeared. Carl looked at Rita and said, "I got the last one. It's your turn!" Rita bit her lip tentatively then slipped in and retrieved the knife before anyone was hurt.

"Chaos" seemed to be the experience that echoed throughout the household of each person I interviewed. Whether we grew up in a large family or we were an only child, our lives felt chaotic. Much of it was from the constant fighting between our parents. My parents didn't fight in front of us, but we felt the constant tension.

My mom and her second husband didn't hold back, though. We usually heard them yelling at each other—their voices escalated just before the thud of something thrown across the room. It was usually Mom lobbing a hairdryer or some other handy object. It was nerve wracking to say the least. I remember an entire day when the fighting was at its worst. Home from college for the weekend, I was awakened by my step-father busting down the front door of the house. Apparently, Mom had changed the locks and he was not happy about it. They fought the entire day. At one point, I gathered up all the guns and knives in the house. I took my brother, sister, and the weapons to some friends of our family for safekeeping. By the end of the day, Mom and her husband had reconciled—leaving us without explanation to deal with the fear, confusion, and anger we felt from being subjected to their behavior.

Coping with all the chaos was no easy task. I remember just trying to keep a low profile so I wouldn't be caught in the cross-fire. Sometimes I would detach from the situation or physically leave the house. As an adult, though, I found myself almost craving chaos in my life and romantic relationships. If things were too stable, I would get bored and create some type of crisis like having an affair—not a coping mechanism I recommend. What I have learned is that stability is a good thing and there are healthy ways to create excitement in your life. These days, if I feel bored with my relationship, I talk about it with my partner. There have been times I learned that they were bored, too. There are many books and people available to help put the spark back into your relationship. If you look at your life and realize that there is a lot of chaos in it, you may want to consider how much you are contributing to the situation. Are you creating a crisis or maybe allowing people in your life to do so?

Now, if I become bored with my life, I think of something I wanted to do as a child. Talking to siblings, cousins, or childhood friends has helped me remember some of those things. Then I go out and do it! So what if it's riding a mini-bike or learning to sky-dive. I have begun to reconnect with my childhood dreams—a very powerful thing to do.

Chapter 7

Emotional Unavailability

*S*arah *was getting ready to move cross-country from her family and hometown. She made an obligatory visit to say goodbye to her mother. "Well, I hope you're happy," her mother said. "You're breaking your mother's heart. I know you're going to fall flat on your face. Don't call me when you do because I'm not the Bank of Mom." Then she said, "Give me a hug" and began to cry. It was very difficult for Sarah to hug her mother because they had never hugged, so it was like hugging a stranger. How sad for this woman who didn't know how to express love for her daughter! How sad for her daughter who felt the need to move so far away in order to find peace!*

❧

I can remember looking into my mom's eyes—searching for something—and realizing that she just wasn't there. She was disconnected; not engaged. She was simply going through the motions of her life. That's why I believe she threw herself into big projects, like finishing college with honors. She could focus on studying and didn't have to feel—she could stay in her head and leave those scary emotions tucked away.

Fortunately, she was good about verbally expressing her love for me. On the other hand, it took me a long time to experience the feeling of love. Even though we said, "I love you" a lot, I didn't know how it *felt* until I was an adult. Maybe it's because I became emotionally disconnected at an early age, too.

Along with the emotional unavailability, there was a certain level of neediness from Mom. My world revolved around her emotional needs. I believe it's because my mom was struggling to survive her disease and it required what little focus she had. Because my mom didn't seek treatment until later in life, after I was grown, her illness went untreated while I was a child. As a result, her mood swings were keeping us both very busy. Although she managed to address my physical needs, she had little emotional support to offer. I believe she would have given it if she could because I remember Mom consoling me at times when I was a child.

As an adult, it has been a challenge to allow myself to receive the emotional support that I need. The first step was to be aware of my needs, which took me years, and then I had to find ways to fulfill those needs. I also pay attention to whether I feel emotionally engaged. It's so easy to dissociate because that's what I did for many years. I don't want to miss any of my life now. Each day offers incredible opportunities and I want to be present for all of them!

Some of us refuse to depend on others for emotional support, but we don't hesitate to be there for everyone else. How can we possibly continue to give support unless we replenish our supply? Make sure you take time to refuel yourself emotionally. That may include taking a walk, reading a book, or just sitting still for a few moments. Allow yourself to feel good about taking care of you!

Chapter 8

Anger and Abuse

When I was twelve years old, my parents got into an intense argument about money. My father lost control and hit Mother so hard that her eyes rolled back in her head. I said to my older sister, "Do something! Don't just stand there! Don't let him do that!" We were all scared, and I knew that my 6-year-old brother couldn't do anything about it. Father was about to hit her again when I ran over and slugged him in the stomach as hard as I could. Of course, he started to come after me. Fortunately, Mother had regained her wits enough to say, "Don't you hurt her!" Some mysterious power came over me and I said, "I'm not afraid of him anymore!" My father stood there staring at me. I just locked eyes with him and refused to look away from his intimidating gaze. He had scared me for the last time. He never again hit my mother—at least not when I was around.

The previous passage is a good example of our parents' outbursts of anger that were common. As a result, life was uncertain and we learned to limit activities such as inviting friends over or just having fun. It was difficult to relax because we never knew when Mom or Dad would become enraged. We never knew what we could share with them in our own experiences because they might over react to an innocent invitation to a dance or the celebration of a team accomplishment, or they might use private information against us in an embarrassing public situation.

Some children of bipolar parents became adults who have difficulty having fun and knowing how it feels to be relaxed. We found ourselves attracted to people with short fuses until we finally realized that we don't have to live our lives in fear and angst.

The physical and emotional abuse endured by some of the people interviewed was especially difficult to hear. To meet most of us CBPs, one would never imagine we had been battered. Most of us are fully functioning adults and lead what appear to be typical lives—even though some of us grew up believing we were stupid, incapable, or unworthy of being loved. We have had to work hard to realize how wrong those beliefs were.

For those of you who did endure the tragedy of physical and severe emotional abuse, I am truly sorry you had to experience something you didn't deserve. I congratulate you for having the courage and ability to survive. Know that you are now safe to discover the bright, extraordinary, authentic person you were always meant to be.

Chapter 9

Searching for Significance

I feel superior and inferior at the same time. Because I excelled in many areas of my life, I developed an elitist attitude. However, my perfectionism never allowed me to feel good enough no matter how much I achieved. My father judged me on the basis of my accomplishments and only showed up when I excelled significantly or achieved something big. With all that I accomplished—captain of an award-winning swim team, top of my class, acceptance into an exclusive university—I have realized that I will never truly please my father. As a result, I feel a sense of insecurity. I believe that success in life, the amount of money I make, and the number of possessions I accumulate define my worth to others.

Our bipolar parents were so busy being in their illness, that it took a lot to get their attention. As a result, we had to perform fantastic feats, good or bad, to get them to notice us. We had to be super athletes or brilliant students, or some of us would get ourselves into trouble so our parent was forced to show up for us. Children want approval from their parents, so we wear ourselves out striving to accomplish great things. If great things don't work, we find more destructive ways to jolt them. We take these behaviors into adulthood and either exhaust ourselves by accomplishing goal after goal or we get stuck in a vicious cycle of problems.

We can break those patterns by letting go of our need to

be legitimized by our parents or by others. Okay, maybe we can't completely let go of this need, but we need to find a way to loosen our grip on it. I still seek validation from trusted friends and from my sister. I also know at a deep level that I am a good person with something to offer *myself* and others— love, friendship, honesty, kindness. I spent many years trying to live up to everyone else's expectations and completely wore myself out. Most of the time I was trying to anticipate those expectations which grew each time I met them! When I began defining the way I wanted to live my life and what brought me happiness, everything around me became brighter, bigger, and more exciting. No one holds me back with their expectations, their fears, or their own disappointments. I hold them in love and know that those are their feelings and experiences. I'm now busy creating my own dreams—it's much more fun.

Be kind to yourself—you may have never done this, but it's absolutely critical. Do something for yourself everyday— something beyond going to work and earning a paycheck or caring for your family. Those are things you do for others. Spend time listening to music that *you* love, visualizing *your* dream life, or relishing one of *your* favorite treats. You will have so much more left to give if you do simple things to replenish your supply of love. You needn't always look to others to do the restocking.

Chapter 10

The Eggshell Syndrome

Higher and higher she bounced. Rita loved to jump on the bed. She felt free and light. Her brother and she laughed and giggled as they sailed higher. Their mother came to the door of the bedroom and watched them. Rita shouted, "Mommy, watch me! I can jump higher than Carl!" Her mother just smiled and walked away. The next day, the two children were having another bounce-fest. They were having so much fun they didn't hear their mother come into the room. Suddenly, Rita felt her mother's vice grip on her arm and the sting of her hand on Rita's bottom. Her laughter choked into tears of shock.

❧

Walking on eggshells seemed to be something we all did as children. Our parents' inconsistent discipline made it very difficult to understand the rules. We operated in a constant state of tension because we never knew what to expect and the boundaries were never clear. An acceptable behavior one day might be punishable the next. The "eggshell syndrome" also stemmed from the unpredictability of our parents' mood swings.

One of the women I interviewed recalled a day when she and her mother worked all day to clean their basement game room so that she could have some friends over. They went to the grocery and bought snacks. The time they spent together was fun. As soon as she and her friends started to have a great time, her mother became enraged and began screaming at her. Of course, her friends didn't know what to think and she was completely humiliated. She never again invited friends to her house.

As parents, CBPs find it challenging not to follow the same pattern. Some have realized the importance of consistently communicating the rules and expectations to our children. We understand that uncertainty in a child's home creates a place that feels unsafe. It's a matter of paying attention to your own behavior and making sure you are consistent with the way you communicate—to everyone in your life, not just your children. Help eliminate the eggshell syndrome from your family and your own life.

Also, remember that you don't have to anticipate everyone's needs. Adults are responsible for communicating their needs. I still sometimes find myself responding the way I think someone wants me to respond or trying guess what someone wants/needs from me. It's challenging to break those patterns that have been with me for a very long time, but I'm ready to retire that well-honed radar. Keeping it sharp has been exhausting!

Chapter 11

Boundary Bullies

W hat the hell is a boundary?" Dana laughed. If you draw a line in the sand with my mother, she will dance all over it, all around it, and wiggle her toes on the line. When she knows the line is there, she becomes like a child taunting to see how far you will let her go.

During spring break one year, I visited the college that a girlfriend attended the prior year. The students had a tradition of painting their bodies and streaking nude across campus. I had never seen anything like it, so I took photos of the hilarious, shocking scene. I put them in a box with other mementos and forgot about them. When I came home after college to live with my mother, I stored some boxes in the garage. Of course, my mother found the pictures during one of her snooping sessions. She never confronted me about the pictures and made her own assumptions. Later she told my sister that I was into some type of deviant sex cult that held orgies! I laughed when I heard the story, but it was a huge invasion of privacy!

❧

How many times have you taken that big risk with your bipolar parent and actually said "no" to them? How many times have you had to stand your ground with your parent after saying no?

As children, we didn't understand the lack of boundaries because it was simply part of our reality that we lived with. People who didn't grow up with a bipolar parent could not fathom their mother or father reading their most personal thoughts written in a journal. They have no idea what it's like to have your parent open your mail or share detailed personal information with a stranger. Most people don't understand why it's so difficult for us to set a boundary and then stand our ground to enforce it. We CBPs must go to extremes and be very diligent to maintain something that others take for granted.

A woman I spoke with related a story about her own struggles with saying "no" to anyone. She was in a therapy session and began to cry when she faced the reality. She said to her therapist, "I know I'm a doormat." Her therapist reached over and gently patted her hand saying, "Honey, you're not a door mat. You're the wall to wall carpeting."

It took me a long time to even realize that I didn't know how to set healthy boundaries. Either I would allow people to take advantage of me or I would push them away completely and shut them out of my life without explaining why. After doing some work around this, I am more aware of situations that feel invasive. I have learned how to gently push back when someone wants more from me than I am willing to give and to be very firm if I have to enforce the boundary.

I tell my mom that I need to get off the phone or that I'm not available to do something for her. She usually respects my requests, but sometimes I do have to remind her. It's easier these days because she's medicated, but I still have to tell her what my needs are and where the lines are drawn as I do with anyone else in my life. It wasn't an overnight change either. The first step was for me to learn how to identify when I needed to set a boundary and then to tell my mom. The first time was scary, but I can't tell you how freeing it was! I claimed my power as a person and never looked back.

Chapter 12

Premature Maturity

I *always felt like the parent in my relationship with my mother even though inside I was such a fragile child. I made sure Mother was safe, and that her needs were taken care of. I tried to joke and have fun with her—even stand on my head if it helped, and sometimes it did. At one point in her life, Mother was very social, and then she became withdrawn. After I was on my own, I would bring my mother along when I went out with my friends. It was never as much fun with her along, but I felt bad because she didn't have friends of her own.*

Many of us took on adult roles and responsibilities at an early age because we didn't have parental guidance or support. We put our own needs aside to care for our parents when they were physically or emotionally ill.

Without anyone realizing it, I decided at the age of four that I needed to put my mother's needs first as much as possible. No one told me to do this, it was simply a child's understanding of how to manage her environment—how to make sure mommy didn't go away again or didn't get upset. As an adult, however, my inability to voice or even be aware of my own needs became extremely dangerous for me. I was so busy taking care of everyone else's emotional needs, I didn't realize that I had spiraled into a depression until I was deep into it.

We're all human systems that need to be fed—physically,

emotionally, mentally, and spiritually. If we only feed others, we eventually deplete our own supply. If you don't eat, you starve to death. If you don't receive love, you know only hate. If you don't challenge your mind, your brain becomes useless. If you're unable to believe in something, you lose hope. My own spiritual malnutrition was the final phase for me. Once I lost faith in humanity, God, and myself there was no reason to live.

After a lifetime of focusing on other's needs, I learned to pay attention to my own. Today, my friends tease me that "it's all about me." There was a time when hearing something like that made me cringe with guilt. I felt selfish, but now I know better. According to the Merriam-Webster Online Dictionary, selfish means, "seeking or concentrating on one's own advantage, pleasure, or well-being without regard for others." I still care about others and I don't take advantage of anyone. On the other hand, I have just as much right as anyone else to have my needs met and there is nothing selfish about that. So, now the "it's all about me" reference is a badge I wear with honor and a smile.

Chapter 13

Manic Manipulation

When my sisters and I began to talk about our childhood memories, we realized that our mother had exhibited certain behaviors, such as her vice grip on our arms, only when she had one of us alone. She also played us against one another saying, "Why can't you be smart like your sister?" As a result, we grew up resenting one another. We didn't begin to talk until we were grown and gone from home—and even then the conversation began by accident. As the information began to flow, we realized that our mother had manipulated us all our lives.

Many of us remember our bipolar parents being manipulative. Sometimes they would confide in us about our other parent or a sibling and pit us against one another. We learned not to talk about what was going on—not even with our own family members. Some of us finally realized, as adults, that it was okay and important to talk. Then, all the lights came on when we realized what our mother or father had done. It's another freeing experience and it can leave you feeling angry. While it's important for you to go with your feelings, getting stuck there will not help you heal. Do whatever you need to move through the anger and forgive your mother or father. Bipolar is an illness, not an excuse. What they did was wrong and it had nothing to do with you. Unfortunately, you bore the brunt of their inappropriate behavior, but you did *not* cause it.

Just because we became adults doesn't mean our parents stopped the manipulative behavior either. After becoming aware, we can at least attempt to set boundaries. Communication is critical—with your mother or father and with your siblings. Talking about your childhood experience with brothers, sisters, aunts, uncles, and cousins will reveal things you never imagined.

Many siblings of bipolar became much closer as adults— the illness that separated us as children brought us together in adulthood.

Chapter 14

Out of Body, Out of Mind

*T*he worst incident I recall was a day when I was thirteen years old. My parents were in the process of separating, so our home life was unstable. I came home from school to find broken glass splashed all over the porch and immediately felt a knot of horror form in my stomach. Something was terribly wrong. As soon as I reached the front door, I was overwhelmed by an odor. The living room was turned upside down. In a fit of rage, my father had thrown a full bottle of bleach all over the furniture. He had pulled the phone out of the wall and thrown it against a bathroom door splintering the wood. It was surprising because my father enjoyed material things, but on that day, he destroyed everything he had worked so hard to attain.

No one was in sight so I began walking through the house calling out for my family. Realizing that no one was home, I walked out the front door and found my father crawling up the sidewalk that led to our house. He was so drunk he couldn't stand up. His hands were bleeding from crawling on the broken glass. It was terrifying. An adult should have been available to calm me and tell me that everything would be okay. My father was in no condition to be the adult. He managed to crawl back into the house and into the bathroom where he vomited. Then he asked me to give him a hidden bottle of bourbon. I was so traumatized at this point that I dissociated. I can't remember how I reunited with my mother and siblings or whether my father was taken to the hospital. My spirit went somewhere away from the situation causing the trauma. The memory is locked away until I feel safe enough *to revisit that horrifying sight of my father torturing himself and destroying our home.*

One coping mechanism that many of us utilized to escape the chaos involved checking out or tuning out the confusion. Many of us don't remember specific experiences in our lives because we just weren't "present" in our bodies. There have been many times when I awakened to find that I was already physically awake, but not emotionally (and sometimes mentally) engaged at all. It was as if my body was a shell, but the essence of me had gone to another place. Sounds familiar—my mother did this, too.

Children use dissociation to survive severe abuse. They create safe havens in their psyche and go there when the abuse becomes too much to bear. Since I'm not aware that I was physically abused, I believe I learned how to dissociate from my mother.

Unfortunately, she wasn't able to continue dissociating—she became too depressed. I did the same. I focused on accomplishing goals that allowed me to stay in my head so that I didn't have to face or even acknowledge the hollowness in my heart. I believe that's why I don't remember a lot of specific childhood or adult experiences. I can recall general ideas about certain times in my life, but there are many memories that simply elude me.

For me, the downside of dissociating was that eventually I had to reconnect or die. Although I'm not bipolar, I have dealt with depression throughout my life and finally hit bottom in 2001. It has been quite a journey and today, I'm grateful for every day because I get another chance to love, learn, and to be loved—by me.

Chapter 15

Financial Frenzy

W**hen I was fourteen, my father confided that the company he worked for owed him money. He said they were going to be sorry for not paying him. He stole a critical piece of system source code he had written and tried to hold it hostage for payment of the money he was owed. You see, he was desperate because he had known for two years that he was going to be prosecuted for stealing $119,000 from another company. He was told that he would only get probation if he could pay $50,000 back, so he believed he had found the perfect solution—extortion from the next employer. It all seemed rational to him.**

The company that owed him money didn't play his game, so he was unable to come up with the money that would keep him out of prison. He was supposed to report to prison on a certain date, but he was convinced that he had received an extension and didn't have to go until later. The police were not so convinced and they came to our house, put him in hand cuffs, and drove him away in the squad car. He was taken to prison where he stayed for seventeen months. I was crushed and felt as though my dad had died.

Although we may not have been fully aware of the financial pressures resulting from our bipolar parents' illness, it was likely a frequent subject of arguments between our parents. Many of our bipolar parents who spent excessively during their manic phases created debt that was very difficult to pay off and may have forced our parents into bankruptcy.

If our parents divorced, it is likely that money was one of the issues. Because a lot of us didn't have positive role models, we may find ourselves in similar situations simply because we weren't taught how to manage our money. Fortunately, I learned the importance of living within my means and not carrying a lot debt—without going through bankruptcy. If you are having difficulty managing your finances, please seek out a professional to help you. There are many wonderful people who have the skills and the desire to teach you how to become a better money manager. You don't need that stress in your life—that was your parent's experience. It does not have to be yours.

Chapter 16

Obsession Confessions

My mother was an obsessive note writer. She loved Post It®
notes and steno notebooks. She would stick these notes all
over the house—directions to places, her calorie record, and
her dog's calorie intake for the last ten years. She died three years ago,
and when my sister and I cleaned her house, there were notes on top of
notes inside her cabinets. Most of the entries in her steno journals were
mundane daily records. Only five lines contained any reference to her
personal thoughts. They revealed that she was lonely and felt trapped
in her disease.

For many of us, the most vivid memory of obsessive
behavior from our mother or father involved cleaning the house.
Because one of our religious holidays precluded us from eating
anything with yeast or rising agents, we cleaned our house from
top to bottom once a year. I never saw any crumbs lurking in
the dark recesses of the kitchen, but I'm sure they were there
and I'm sure they would have sent us to hell if we hadn't cleaned
them out!

Bipolar disorder is all about extremes. The highs are
intoxicating and lows are debilitating. As a result, people with
bipolar seem to only understand excessiveness. When we began
to celebrate Christmas again, my mother wrapped all the gifts in
matching paper with coordinating bows. Here's my confession—
I do it, too. Her Christmas tree looked like something out of a
magazine—absolutely beautiful and perfect!

The obsessions can take many forms and leave their own marks. When he was a boy, one of the people I interviewed had to pick up sticks around the yard and put them into small piles that he then had to consolidate into large piles. His father would check his work to make sure he had done everything correctly. Because children carry into adulthood the behaviors we learned from our parents, we may have some of those same obsessions. I don't think Drake picks up sticks in the yard anymore, but he is a perfectionist. There was a time when I refused to admit that I was, but now realize that I do need things a certain way. There is nothing wrong with being a perfectionist—unless you take it to such an extreme that it disrupts yours or someone else's life.

Childhood is just the beginning, but what an important part of life it is! Those experiences lay the foundation for the issues we spend at least part of our adult lives working through. It usually comes down to information and our willingness to look honestly at ourselves. Your life will be much more fulfilling if you can get beyond your parent's behavior and focus on your life. It is your life after all. You deserve to have whatever you desire—loving relationships, stability, joyful work, peace! Your childhood can only keep you from these things if you allow it. The next section of the book presents steps you can take in order to understand your parent's behavior and, in turn, begin your healing process.

PART FOUR

MAGNIFICENT MAPS

Chapter 17

So, What Am I?

This chapter is the most challenging one for me to write. The difficulty lies in the honest introspection that I must do to write it.

My mother is bipolar. So, what am I?

I am an infant born into this world *five* weeks later than expected. I have wondered if I was trying to negotiate a different contract with God. Some part of me must have known what I was getting myself into. Nonetheless, I came into this world and began a journey.

I am a child who took on adult responsibilities at a very young age. The consequences of bearing this emotional load of the adults around me were subtle, but it dealt a hefty punch to my psyche. It's not a birth order thing as I once believed because my siblings felt the same pressure and responsibility. At different times in our lives, we were left to fend for ourselves and to take care of Mom's needs. I constantly "scanned" my environment with well-honed radar and made the necessary shifts so that Mom and other loved ones would be happy with me. As a result, I was so busy making sure everything and everyone else was okay that it was difficult to take care of my needs. I simply ignored my feelings.

I am the teenager of a broken home who faced puberty in an unfamiliar city. The awkwardness of that age was kicked up several notches by significant changes for my family when I was twelve. My parents divorced. My mother remarried. We moved to Nashville and away from our family. Simply adjusting to the changes in my body would have been enough to keep me busy, but dealing with all those other big changes was too much. I just shut down.

I am the young woman who chose to follow my mother's dream career because I didn't have the nerve to follow my own. During my senior year of high school, I remember talking with my mother for hours about what I wanted to do with my life. She tried to help me look at various fields that I could pursue. In my heart, I wanted to be a writer and a teacher, but because those fields weren't known for producing a lucrative income, we didn't spend much time discussing them. So, to please my mom, I decided to get an accounting degree. I struggled through most of the classes, and managed to graduate. After dedicating myself to a challenging corporate career for twenty years and achieving some success, God decided it was time for me to follow my dream. I finally got the message after being laid off twice in two years.

I am the woman who continued to ignore my own needs in order to take care of those I loved. I abandoned myself. The result was disastrous and almost fatal. I was attracted to people who knew exactly what they wanted in life. It was very comforting to be with someone so confident. It was easy to grab hold of their ideals and make them mine. I busied myself helping them make their dreams come true and stopped dreaming myself. Instead, my goals looked a lot like theirs. I became very good at achieving goals that were really someone else's. I learned how to climb the corporate ladder, make good money, and acquire nice things. The problem was that after many years, I lost touch with my heart and finally realized that I had no clue what I wanted or how I felt about many things. I believe this intensified the depression that had begun to seep into my life.

I am a child of a bipolar mother and I struggled for many years with setting healthy boundaries. I went from never saying "no" to my mom to virtually cutting myself off from her. I knew what I was doing, but I didn't realize that the core issue was related to boundaries. My behavior carried over into my friendships. I would take a lot of crap from someone until they did something, probably trivial, that sent me over the edge and I would end the friendship. Many times I wouldn't communicate why—the relationship would simply be finished. Setting boundaries is something I still work on today. I know that I am worthy of having boundaries and I understand my responsibility in expressing my needs. I'm learning that people are willing to respect my requests—it's a powerful feeling—not in a negative, controlling way, but in a validating way.

I am a person who had no information about what was going on around and within me. As a result, I viewed bipolar disorder and depression as mental illnesses that didn't happen in my family. Part of my stigma was related to my mother's experience with ineffective treatments. I now understand that she wasn't being treated for the correct illness—an illness that was properly diagnosed years ago, but one she didn't accept due to the stigma she held about bipolar disorder. Her belief was that people with bipolar disorder were crazy, so she couldn't possibly be bipolar because she wasn't crazy!

I am a woman who went to the very edge of darkness and looked over the cliff. I suffered far too long due to my own prejudices about mental illness, including depression. By the grace of some mighty spiritual force, I didn't jump off the cliff. Instead, I reclaimed my own spirit and now live every day with absolute joy!

I am the daughter who, at the mid-point of my life, is finally able to enjoy a healthy relationship with my mother. Both of us have worked very hard to get where we are today. Since accepting her diagnosis, my mother has stayed on her medications, even when they didn't seem to make her feel better. She stuck with the treatment until the doctor was able to get the correct mix and dosages that stabilized her condition. I now have learned to express my needs and set healthy boundaries with Mom, and she respects those boundaries. I no longer resent my mother for the past and appreciate those experiences that taught me so much. I am also more tolerant and aware of what my mother is going through. I understand when she calls and talks a mile a minute about everything. I know she is manic or hypomanic and I just listen. Getting to this point has not been easy for either of us. It has taken a huge commitment to take care of ourselves and the result has been well worth the effort.

I am a better daughter, sister, friend, partner because of my experience and the work I have done to build the life that is truly mine.

I am a very happy, hopeful, positive person who wants to help erase the stigma that keeps people from seeking treatment. Removing the stigma of mental illness is so important— particularly for depression and bipolar. People are dying from a lack of information. In our stress-filled society, more people try to push through without seeking help. If they knew how much better they would feel with proper treatment, we would be a far more stable race. Because they lack information about the symptoms brought on by a chemical imbalance, they don't realize that there is hope and there is a solution. Death is not the only alternative to relieving our pain.

Chapter 18

Understanding Leads to Better Coping

When you were a child, did you realize that something was different about your parent? If so, did you have any idea what to call it? Most of us had no language for discussing those differences that we noticed. No one talked about mental illness unless it was in reference to some other poor family. Maybe we just made comments like "Oh, that's crazy Uncle Joe" or "We need to be very quiet. Mother is having one of her spells." Without the information or the language to discuss bipolar disorder, we didn't know that our loved one could get help or that our lives could have been different. The lack of information and the stigma attached to mental illness made a significant difference in our world. Too many families have endured years of silent anguish and ignorance. My mother certainly didn't want to be labeled as a manic-depressive or bipolar. Therefore, she refused her first bipolar diagnosis. Who knows what her life would look like now if she had accepted it the first time?

Although bipolar disorder involves behavioral symptoms, it is caused by a chemical imbalance. It is similar to cancer, diabetes or any other physical illness; the earlier your loved one receives proper treatment, the better their chances are for a stable, productive life. If your parent denies or refuses to get help, the problem will likely become worse and could result in hospitalization, self-harm, or suicide.

Bipolar disorder is still misunderstood by most of society.

There are people who still hold the belief that a bipolar person is dangerous and should be locked in a padded cell. As a result, you may be hesitant to discuss your parent's disorder with friends, family members, or co-workers for fear that they may judge you. If they do, it is probably because they are ignorant on the subject. I urge you not to allow another's lack of knowledge keep you or your loved one from seeking the help that will improve (and possibly save) your life.

The more I talk with people about bipolar disorder, the more I realize how many families are affected by it. While in the salon recently, I mentioned this book to my hair stylist. I told her that I had interviewed several people and heard some very interesting stories about those who either had the disorder themselves or knew someone with bipolar. When she asked me to give some examples, everyone in the salon fell silent and all eyes were suddenly on me. The customers eagerly waited to hear me tell more. I suspect they were reflecting on their own experiences and asking themselves whether there might be hints of bipolar disorder in their own families. It occurred to me that mental illness, bipolar disorder in particular, is a hot topic these days. There must be a high number of people who tolerate it—a lot more than the two percent reported in America. I believe there are many people who have not been diagnosed or received treatment, and, as a result, suffer needlessly.

Three Steps Forward

Your healing journey will not likely be an overnight trip. You will be stepping out of your comfort zone—over and over again. You will be challenging your belief system. You will experience some guilt, anger, and sadness, and you will make some difficult decisions along the way. As you make the journey, know that your hard work will result in a huge improvement in your life.

Here are three steps to follow in making your journey. These are the "accidental" steps that I took to work through my frustration with my mother and to build a better relationship with her. The three steps are (1) talk about your experience, (2) learn about bipolar disorder, and (3) watch for shifts in your parent's behavior.

Talk About Your Experience

I believe that talking about our childhood experiences is vital to our healing process. I'm not saying you need to go back and relive every unpleasant experience. Simply acknowledge the impact those experiences had on your life and the behaviors you picked up as a result. Find someone you trust—a sibling, family member, therapist, anyone—and talk with them about your memories and feelings. Allow yourself to understand the impact your parent's behavior and choices had on you. If you don't feel you have anyone you can trust, then write about your experience. No one else needs to see what you have written, and putting your thoughts on paper will help you see the affect.

The people who shared their stories told me that discussing their feelings with other family members revealed a lot to them. They realized that their siblings had similar experiences and resentments due to being pitted against one another by their parent. After they began to talk, walls that had existed for many years began to melt and new bonds were formed. They were able to support one another as they began to look at their own behaviors and improve their lives.

When you are ready, talk with your parent about their illness. If your parent has been diagnosed, you should be able to speak more openly with them because they will have some understanding of their illness. You can ask them what it's like to experience their cycles of mania and depression. Make sure you have the discussion while your parent is stable so you get a more realistic response from them. Find out whether they are being treated by a psychiatrist and a therapist. If so, get the names of the practitioners. This is important because you may want to talk with them at some point, with your parent's permission, so you can understand their treatment program.

If your parent has not been diagnosed or doesn't accept their diagnosis, wait until you have learned more about the disorder. As you develop a better understanding, you will be able to sense the best time to talk with your parent and the best way to have the discussion. Make sure that you speak in a non-defensive manner. Your parent may become defensive, but you want to stay calm. The purpose of beginning the dialog is to help both of you get beyond the guilt and shame to build a healthier relationship based on respect and trust.

Whether your family members realized it, your parent's illness had a tremendous impact on your family unit. When your parent is diagnosed, there will likely be some fall out. Since people with untreated bipolar disorder usually exhibit some form of hypochondria or psychosis, family members may have become impatient or unsupportive over the years. Those same family members may feel guilty upon learning that their parent is truly ill. If they try to compensate for any wrongdoing, it may affect their ability to set boundaries and realistic expectations with their parent. You and your siblings may be concerned that you will inherit the illness, or you may be tempted to forsake your own life pursuits in an effort to look after your parent.

You can overcome these challenges and get through the difficult moments. You have taken the first step by reading this book.

If you feel comfortable doing so, talk with a healthcare professional—your doctor, a therapist/counselor, or a psychiatrist who specializes in treating bipolar disorder. You may have a lot of questions about your parent, bipolar disorder, and yourself. Seeking information from the professionals is a great way to learn. It doesn't mean you need to be treated by them—unless you want to.

Learn About Bipolar Disorder

After you begin to talk about your own experience, the next step is to educate yourself about your parent's illness. Although I have provided basic information in this book, there are many other helpful, practical resources available to you. Some of these resources are listed in Appendix A.

A guide entitled, *The Intelligent Patient Overview* provides a detailed look at bipolar disorder and includes information about the common signs and symptoms, methods used to establish the diagnosis, standard treatments, available treatment options, promising new developments, quality of life issues, and questions to ask your parent's doctor.

Reading about bipolar disorder is only one way to learn about the symptoms and other aspects of the disease. However, talking with healthcare professionals and other bipolar patients will provide you with up-to-date clinical data and real life information. The Depression Bipolar Support Alliance (DBSA) is a wonderful resource for finding support groups and relevant information that will help you understand your parent's illness. I encourage you to attend a few support group meetings. I found that people at these meetings were very willing to share their experience—they are the experts because they live with the disease. They can also provide you with names of doctors or other healthcare professionals who specialize in treating bipolar patients. See Appendix B for information about how to find a DBSA or other support groups in your area.

The healthcare professionals are a great source also. They can provide you with insight into the various ways bipolar disorder shows up for people. Although I provided a list of symptoms, the disease tends to be different for each person. By talking with someone who specializes in bipolar disorder, you can get a broader perspective of the illness. You will likely come away with information that will allow you to view your parent in a new light.

Although some people reject a bipolar diagnosis due to the stigma associated with it, many people receive it with a sigh of relief. They are happy to finally know that the ups and downs they have been experiencing are really periods of "mania" and "depression" caused by an illness that can be treated.

After receiving the manic-depressive diagnosis from her psychiatrist, Patty Duke wrote in her book: *A Brilliant Madness—Living with Manic-Depressive Illness,* "...the words just made sense. As my psychiatrist said them, I remember nodding my head as if I had known this all along. They are the best two words I ever heard. They described how it felt to be me."

In addition to feeling relieved, a bipolar person may also feel guilty for past behavior, being a burden to the family, increased medical and credit card bills, their difficultly in holding a job, or continual disruptions in the household. They may feel that they have let everyone down. The good news is that the proper diagnosis is the first step in regaining stability and productivity in their life.

Watch For It

Because of the related stigma, your mother or father may go untreated for years without seeking help or wanting to deal with their symptoms. You can provide valuable support to your parent and your family simply by learning how to identify the symptoms of bipolar disorder and watching for warning signs of recurrent manic or depressive episodes. The symptoms vary from one individual to another, but there are some common signs of both depressive and manic states. You can create a checklist from the depressive and manic symptoms provided in Chapter 3 of this book. Share the checklist with your family members and ask them whether they have witnessed any of the symptoms. If you notice a combination of symptoms, I suggest that you contact your parent's doctor as quickly as possible to inform them of your observations. If your loved one is having thoughts of suicide, take them seriously. Get them to the emergency room, call 9-1-1, contact a medical professional, or use a crisis hotline (800-442-HOPE).

There are several factors that may trigger a mood swing: a biological cycle, anniversary dates, holidays, stress, belief systems, bad news, or tragic world events. Many bipolar people have a regular biological rhythm to their mood swings—their cycles may be seasonal or cyclical. An episode may be triggered by the anniversary date of a remembered trauma or significant event such as divorce, death of a loved one, relocation, or a previous occurrence of mania or depression. Holidays can be stressful for everyone, but even more so for your bipolar mother or father. It is a time of family gatherings that may be accompanied by guilt for past behavior or tension with unsupportive family members.

Stressful life events (even some you would consider positive) that deviate from your parent's routine may be a trigger. If your parent believes that an episode is inevitable or that they have no control, chances are the prediction will be fulfilled. For some bipolar people, hearing bad news or watching tragic events on television (such as terrorism or natural disaster) may be upsetting enough to trigger an episode.

You have probably experienced the long phone calls from your parent whenever they are manic, or you likely cannot find them when they are depressed. Your ability to observe shifts in your parent's behavior will make your life much easier. You can either get your parent to the doctor or take a break from contact with them if they refuse treatment. The important thing is to understand your parent's symptoms so you can make informed decisions.

Chapter 19

Dispelling the Myths

Although we have begun to hear more about bipolar disorder, depression and other mental illnesses, many people still hold images of a mentally ill person as one tortured by demons, or someone who exhibits violent behavior, or a shell of a person roaming the halls of a mental institution. These opinions might be derived from movies and literature that dramatized and sensationalized mental illness. Most people fear what they do not understand. This seems especially true with mental illness, since those who live with it every day have just recently begun to talk openly about it. Still, some of those who do talk about it may have little or no information to support their opinion. The widespread assumptions overlook the fact that as many as eighty percent of the people suffering from mental illness are in touch with reality most of the time and can lead normal, productive lives if they receive the appropriate treatment.

A survey based on telephone interviews conducted in the U.S. in 1999 showed that, while general awareness of the physiological nature of bipolar disorder has increased from thirty-six to sixty-three percent over the past four years, perceptions and attitudes toward bipolar disorder have improved very little. Most people know that bipolar disorder is characterized by mood swings and are aware of the telltale signs of depression, but less than half of those surveyed were able to identify symptoms of mania. After being informed of the symptoms, forty-six percent then said they knew someone who exhibited signs of manic-depression. When asked if they would consult a mental health professional or seek help for a loved one they believed was experiencing symptoms of manic-depression, sixty-five percent said they would not. This is a disturbing statistic. Why wouldn't a person reach out to help a loved one? It's all about the stigma that remains so strong.

Forty-four percent believed that people with manic depression were often violent. Eleven percent of the U.S. population believes that mental illness is an emotional shortcoming or character weakness that could be prevented by adopting "self-help" techniques or positive thinking. Most Americans do not realize that bipolar disorder, like heart disease or diabetes, is a physical illness requiring medical treatment. This lack of understanding means that many people are not seeking treatment, and that is especially frightening since depression is at a crisis level in the United States. In order to address some aspects of the stigma attached to bipolar disorder, this chapter will address some of the related myths and provide a more realistic answers.

MYTH: Since my parent is bipolar, I will become bipolar.

TRUTH: While it is true that relatives of people suffering from bipolar illness are ten to twenty times more likely to develop depression or bipolar disorder than the general population, only two of the eighteen (11%) CBPs interviewed for this book were bipolar. Also, four people had been diagnosed with depression. There may be a higher possibility than if your parent wasn't bipolar, but it is not definite.

MYTH: People can "catch" bipolar disorder from others.

TRUTH: While surveys show that twenty-one percent of the population would feel uncomfortable being in the presence of a manic-depressive person, there is absolutely no evidence that bipolar disorder is contagious. The only way you can "catch" it is through your DNA.

MYTH: If someone is diagnosed with bipolar disorder, they may have to spend their life in a mental institution.

TRUTH: A vast majority of people with bipolar are not

treated in a hospital. Some people are admitted to a hospital when they do not respond to normal treatment, or in the event of an episode so severe they are unable to care for themselves. With appropriate treatment, most bipolar people live normal productive lives.

MYTH: People with bipolar disorder will try to commit suicide.

TRUTH: While it is a risk for people with bipolar disorder, not everyone with the illness attempts suicide. It is important for bipolar patients to remain on their treatment programs and have a support team to help them watch for the onset of manic and depressive phases.

MYTH: People with bipolar disorder are unable to keep a job.

TRUTH: Bipolar people are some of the most talented and creative people, and are quite able to succeed in life. They have the potential to work at any level depending upon their own abilities, experience, and motivation. As long as they remain alert to their feelings and behavior and continue appropriate treatment, bipolar people make significant contributions to society as a whole.

MYTH: People diagnosed with bipolar disorder can "snap out of it" if they try hard enough to modify their behavior.

TRUTH: Bipolar disorder is a physical disease just like diabetes or a heart condition. It is *not* a reflection of their character. Their brain chemistry is simply out of balance and can be treated with a well-rounded treatment program that should include medication and talk therapy.

MYTH: Bipolar people frequently lose their temper over trivial things.

TRUTH: Mood swings and personal disposition vary from one person to the next even for those who do not have bipolar disorder. Approximately twenty percent of bipolar people have difficulty controlling their temper. It is, therefore, unfair to create a prejudice against the other eighty percent of bipolar people who are equally and often better able to control their temper than the rest of the population. Again, it is also important for someone with bipolar disorder to actively manage their illness and receive proper treatment.

MYTH: Bipolar people are dangerous.

TRUTH: The majority of people with bipolar disorder are *not* violent. The cases involving violent behavior typically occur when the person feels threatened or is using alcohol or drugs to self-medicate. Bipolar people are just as safe as the majority of the population.

MYTH: Bipolar people are abusive to their children.

TRUTH: As you read in these stories, some form of verbal or emotional abuse showed up in each family. Some children experienced sexual and physical abuse as well. The most severe cases were those in which the parent had not been diagnosed or was not consistently adhering to their treatment program. Parents who are bipolar today may have an advantage over people trying to parent in the past few decades because there is more information available. If a parent is willing to learn about the illness and seek treatment, they will greatly enhance the lives of their children.

The main thing to remember about stigma and misperception is that ignorance is NOT bliss—it is dangerous. Iris Chang was the 36-year-old author of the best-selling book, *The Rape of Nanking*. She had been diagnosed with bipolar disorder prior to the self-inflicted gunshot wound that took her life in 2004. She refused to take medication and asked her family to remain quiet about her illness. Her family believes her suicide could have been prevented if she had taken her medication. The stigma related to bipolar disorder is very strong in the Asian-American community. Her death has had an impact on the community and has motivated Chang's parents and her brother. In hopes of preventing other families from having to experience such a tragedy, they are promoting mental health awareness among Chinese-Americans by raising funds to provide scholarships for Chinese-speaking students who are working toward careers in mental health.

Taking medication also has its stigma. Many people believe that the need to take medicine for bipolar disorder is a sign of weakness and they would feel embarrassed if others knew. I believe this is one reason many bipolar people stop taking their medication or refuse to get help. Another reason is the effectiveness of the drugs. It is sometimes a hassle to take meds and it's tempting to stop taking them if you feel great. However, remind your parent that the medication is the reason they feel so good and that consistent treatment is the key to sustaining that wonderful feeling.

Well intentioned friends who are not properly informed can wreak havoc on a bipolar person's life. My bipolar friend had been going to counseling, taking her meds and doing great until her very "enlightened" friend made a negative comment about people who depended on medication of any kind. To her friend, it was a sign that there were unresolved issues and repressed emotions that she wasn't willing to deal with. Even though my friend was stable and had made great progress in her healing journey, she stopped taking her meds. She didn't want to feel inferior to her friend who seemed to have her act together. The next thing I knew my friend was suicidal. This was after her manic phase during which she began a relationship that quickly became sexual. She was excited about the new love and enjoyed the romantic high, but soon she plummeted into depression. For the first time, she considered the affect the other relationship was having on her marriage and the guilt fueled her downward spiral. She started taking her meds again, but found that they weren't working as well as before. Her doctor doubled the dosage and prescribed an additional medication to get her back on track. About three months later, she was coming out of the depressive phase and made the difficult decision to let go of the friendship that had caused her to relapse. Although she accepts responsibility for not taking her medication, she also realizes that her illness requires a lot of support and that she must surround herself with people who understand her illness and respect her needs.

People have begun to take action to remove the stigma associated with bipolar disorder. AdFilmTies Inc. is a media production company whose goal is to improve the lives of those living with mental illness. AdFilmTies calls upon the general public along with the advertising and film industries to help produce nationally distributed feature films that better support our communities. Their first feature film, *Manic Ride*, tells the story of how bipolar disorder affects an entrepreneur and his family. Screenwriter John DeTitta based the script on his personal experiences in successfully treating and living with bipolar disorder. His hope is that this film will be the most powerful medium for creating awareness and acceptance of mental health issues into the mainstream consciousness of the general public. It's up to all of us to educate ourselves and others about bipolar disorder so people recognize it. Heightened awareness will lead to less prejudice and fear which will help reduce the stigma.

PART FIVE

DIVINE DESTINATIONS

Chapter 20

Setting Boundaries & Voicing Your Needs

Recently, my mother began having more difficulty with her short-term memory and she was experiencing a lot of confusion. Her friend, George, and I accompanied her on a trip to see her psychiatrist. I have to tell you—it was scary for me. For many years, I have been adamantly against becoming involved with my mother's care—whether it involved her physical or mental health. As a child, I didn't have a choice. If Mom was sick, it was up to me to take care of her and my younger siblings. Since becoming an adult with choices, I have opted to stay as far away from that role as possible.

On the other hand, I know more now. I am aware of shifts in my mother's behavior. Instead of thinking she's acting weird in order to manipulate me or others, I understand that, for some reason, she has come out of a stable mode. In the end, George and I were able to provide some very useful information to Dr. Friedman that Mom had forgotten to share or hadn't been able to share. We also learned that he had "tweaked" her medications a couple of months prior to our visit. This may have been the catalyst for the shift in her behavior. I have begun to understand, first hand, how important it is to have some knowledge of my mother's treatment program.

This chapter will discuss ways you can build a healthier relationship with your parent, if you wish to maintain contact with your parent. We will also discuss effective ways to care for your bipolar parent. Let's start by looking at three levels of involvement you might choose to have with your mother or father:

Primary Caregiver: You take responsibility for every aspect of your parent's well-being.

Support System Member: You are there when you can be, but responsibility is shared amongst family members, friends, and professionals. You let your parent care for him/herself when you know they are able.

No Involvement: You have no contact whatsoever with your bipolar parent. Out of necessity for your own well-being, you have had to cut ties.

If you have chosen to be the primary caregiver, it is extremely important that you become as informed as possible. You also need to be capable of setting strong boundaries and reinforcing them. Because we were raised by our bipolar parents, most of us have difficulty taking care of our own needs. Please make sure you are in a healthy place emotionally before you decide to take on this daunting role. Support and assistance from your family members is also critical to ensure your continued well-being along with your parent's. Later in this chapter, you will find more information to help you provide constant support for your parent.

If you are a member of your mother or father's support system, you are like many CBPs. You prefer to support your parent from a healthy distance while maintaining your own life. Your bipolar parent can do most things for him/herself and you may only need to stay in contact enough to monitor changes in their behavior and watch for symptoms. If your bipolar parent is unable to function on their own, you will need to rely on your family members, home healthcare providers, social caseworkers or other professionals. You want to ensure the load doesn't fall completely on any one person's shoulders. If you don't utilize other people to help, you will likely burnout, which helps no one.

If you have already cut ties with your bipolar parent, you may find yourself looking back at times. You may feel guilty for your decision or you may question whether you did the right thing. It takes a strong determination and the ability to set boundaries to move away from a situation that is harmful to you or your family. Only you can make the decision that is right for you. Regardless of whether you remain in contact with your bipolar parent, it is still useful to be informed about bipolar disorder. It will help you to recognize symptoms in your other family members.

More Information for the Primary Caregiver and the Support System

Managing your bipolar parent's life means there will be some rough days. You will need to understand how to navigate the murky waters of medications, psychotherapy, and medical insurance along with other uncharted territories. I'm not telling you this to scare you. I simply want to make sure you take on the responsibility with open eyes. The good news is that you have a lot of resources available to help you.

Start by talking about your parent's illness with your family. This allows everyone to express their concerns, process their feelings, and help determine ways to avoid or minimize the impact of another episode. Plan time for a family discussion and bring your own list of concerns and observations to the table. One of the first things you want to do is educate yourself. As I discussed in the previous chapter, learn all you can about bipolar disorder, its treatment, and ongoing research; and share new information with your family.

Another area you will want to discuss is the level of personal responsibility. As the Primary Caregiver, you will literally become your parent's manager. You have to monitor their condition and know how to support them in the event they are unable to function on their own. In order for you to stay healthy, family members will need to do their part to lessen the burden on you as the primary caregiver. If you are the only person available to look after your parent, I strongly suggest that you obtain help from health care professionals. You will need a periodic break in order to take care of your own needs. Hopefully, you have supportive friends and family because it will be easier for you to take the necessary measures to prevent your own burnout and exhaustion.

Regardless of the severity of your parent's condition, it is important that they work with a team of professionals including a physician, psychiatrist, psychologist, pharmacist, and a social worker skilled in the treatment of bipolar disorder. They can provide you, your parent, and your family with relevant information along with additional approaches to treatment. Take care that your parent is working with one pharmacist so that one professional has full knowledge of all your parent's medications. This will also make it easier for you to maintain a list of the medications should you need it. Having a complete list of your parent's meds will help manage them on a daily basis, and it can be a lifesaver to other caregivers when you are taking those much needed breaks or are unavailable for some reason.

There are certain aspects of bipolar disorder (genetics, physical condition, etc.) that your parent cannot control, but there are behaviors they can modify to prevent or minimize the impact of an episode. Medication alone may not prevent every episode, but it certainly helps keep them to a minimum. When a bipolar person is in a neutral, manic, or hypomanic state, they feel great and may convince themselves that they are cured. Warning! They may stop taking their medications without your knowledge. Therefore, you may need to monitor your bipolar parent's medications to ensure they continue to take them as prescribed.

Another vital topic for family discussion is "what if." Since you can't predict when or if an episode is going to occur, family members must continually anticipate a change in mood or a return of symptoms. If you've ever tried to discuss these things with your parent while they were in the middle of an episode, you know how difficult it can be to obtain the cooperation you need. The time between episodes is an ideal time to plan for the next one. Discuss what you would do should your parent lose their job, express inappropriate behavior, or become violent. Include your parent in determining what you would do if they refused to go to the doctor. Consider when you would decide that your parent needed to go to the hospital, and which hospital or treatment facility they prefer.

You will also need to be familiar with your parent's bills and when they are to be paid. Depending on how severe and debilitating your parent's condition, you may want to get power of attorney, signed medical information release forms, documents for medical leave or disability benefits before another incident occurs. You may also want to discuss what you would do should your parent lose insurance coverage. In severe cases of recurrent rapid cycles, your parent may reach a point where they are unable to care for themselves. This is something you may want to discuss with your mother/father. Due to the significance of a simple change in routine, your plans for a vacation should be discussed well in advance during a stable period so that your parent feels secure.

Developing a plan to prevent another episode is probably one of the most important topics of family discussion. The best way to prevent or minimize the impact of an episode is to learn from previous experience. While your parent is in a stable condition, establish a contract with them that obtains his or her cooperation and permission should you need to intervene. Intervention may involve you providing feedback to your parent regarding changes you notice in their mood and behavior, calling the doctor, taking your parent to the hospital, or reducing stress in their household or work activities.

If you notice symptoms, you will want to say calmly to your mother or father something like, "You seem nervous and preoccupied. Let's sit down and talk about it." Remind them of the contract, but don't push. Discuss choices and options, and suggest modifications that have worked in the past such as reducing stimulation, taking medication, staying on a regular sleep schedule. Be positive and try to keep your sense of humor. When something works, make a note of it and try it again!

Working with Healthcare Professionals

Most of us have been trained since childhood to respect doctors and to trust them as the absolute medical authority.

However, be aware that a lot of them simply don't have practical experience working with someone who has bipolar disorder. Trusting your parent's health issues to a physician who is unknowledgeable about bipolar disorder is very risky and not advised.

Many physicians are quick to prescribe anti-depressant medications for depression; however, if your parent is really bipolar and simply showing signs of depression at the moment, the treatment could make their symptoms worse. Most primary care physicians do not know to ask questions or probe for clues about the manic phases. This means you cannot assume that a physician or therapist will detect bipolar disorder, particularly in its early stages. Non-specialists may not be informed about the latest research studies or treatments. Don't be afraid to interview your parent's doctors. Make sure these practitioners have extensive backgrounds in treating bipolar disorder patients.

Informed people who are most often around someone with bipolar disorder are very likely to recognize symptoms of the illness long before a physician or counselor sees them. Therefore, your observations and other information related to your parent's illness will be extremely valuable to their mental healthcare team. It is also important for your parent to take personal responsibility for their treatment program. They should understand the side effects of prescribed medication before they begin taking a new medicine. Your mother or father should also be educated about their illness so they can monitor their own behavior whenever possible. It is up to them to ask questions and inform their practitioners about symptoms, side effects they experience, or changes in their health. If you accompany your parent to their doctor appointments, openly share any information regarding your parent's behavior, appetite, sleep patterns, etc. Write down any questions you want to ask before the next appointment. A physician will most likely spend more time than usual with a person who arrives with a list of specific questions. Your parent may actually receive better care from a physician who knows that someone is looking out for them. You may be able to remember specific instances, or record important information the physician offers. Ask about newer treatments and if they would be suitable for your parent, especially if there are distressing side effects with their current medication. Ask a physician or pharmacist for information leaflets about various medications for bipolar disorder.

If your parent's current treatment is working well, then beware of anyone who wishes to tamper with the dosage or change a medication. I have learned with my mother that it can take years to get just the right dosage and mix of mood stabilizers, anti-depressants, or anti-seizure medications for her to reach a stable state. It only takes a month or so after making a change in that cocktail to throw her into state of confusion and depression. My advice is for you to request that the physician provide you with a copy of any and all changes to your parent's medicine/treatment. If anything ever looks strange to you, ask questions. Most bipolar people appreciate the idea that another person may be able to pick up on problems before they grow unstable.

If you are not satisfied with the doctor's diagnosis or ability, find another physician with experience in the treatment of bipolar disorder. Please don't wait until your parent gets very sick. Everyone in your family will benefit from your parent receiving the best of mental healthcare. Don't worry about hurting a physician's feelings or that you are showing disrespect. Truth be known, the he or she will probably be relieved.

We understand that bipolar disorder is a long-term illness, and symptoms often relapse. As a caregiver, you will be called upon to assist with long-term preventive treatment to keep your parent's disease under control.

You, your mother or father, and your family have endured a very difficult condition. You withstood the unpredictable forces of bipolar. You and your parent have made tough decisions about your lives. You have taken huge steps by trying to understand a difficult illness. You have survived—it's your time to thrive!

Now that you have a life raft for preserving your sanity, and you know that you are not alone, let's

look at what the future holds for bipolar disorder.

Chapter 22

Bipolar Today and Tomorrow

The intention of this chapter is to provide you with a glimpse of available treatments and to take a look at the future. We'll discuss progress that has been made in diagnosing bipolar disorder, medical treatments that have emerged, non-drug therapies that enhance other treatments, useful tools for managing the condition, and new technologies that are currently being tested.

Diagnosis

There is still a lot of guesswork in diagnosing bipolar disorder. Since there are no tests available to determine brain chemical levels, trial and error is still part of the process of diagnosing and prescribing medication for the disease.

Sometimes a person must become psychotic (exhibit a fundamental mental derangement characterized by defective or lost contact with reality) before doctors are able to determine they are bipolar. However, the mental health community continues to create better tools that enable healthcare professionals to diagnosis bipolar disorder much sooner, which in turn means earlier treatment and saved lives. As these professionals become aware of the need to gather more than superficial information about a potential bipolar patient, more and more people will receive an accurate diagnosis much earlier than in the past.

Bipolar disorder cannot be diagnosed with a blood test or

brain scan. I was surprised to learn this as I began to search for information about bipolar disorder. I didn't understand this since many of the other physiological diseases, like diabetes, can be detected with some sort of blood test. Bipolar diagnoses are still based on the patient's answers to questions and on behavior observed by the doctor. I was told that a more technical means of detection hasn't been developed because our brain chemistry is almost as unique as our DNA or our fingerprints. It is impossible to create one generic test capable of analyzing the monoamine levels in an individual's brain to determine whether their levels are consistent with bipolar patients. However, it seems that some progress has been made toward developing a detection tool with the positron emission tomography (PET) brain imaging technique referenced in Chapter 3. I believe scientists will fine-tune this tool so it can be used to help a lot of people get the proper diagnosis and treatment as earlier as possible. We aren't quite there yet.

Medical Treatments

Because its exact cause has not been determined, there is no known method to prevent or cure bipolar disorder. As a result, the physicians are left with treating it with available medications.

As you may already know from witnessing the effect on your parent, continual treatment is more effective than an on-off approach. However, since individuals respond differently to medications, it may take some trial-and-error to stabilize someone who has just been diagnosed or who has stopped taking their meds. The drugs lose their effectiveness if your parent starts and stops taking them.

Twenty years ago, lithium was about the only medication thought to be effective in treating bipolar. Today, there are a number of medications including a whole new generation of antidepressants, anticonvulsant drugs, and mood stabilizers. Most people with bipolar disorder take more than one medication. For instance, my mother is on six different medications that treat her disorder. She takes two mood stabilizers, one anti-depressant medication, one anti-anxiety drug, and one sleeping pill. She also takes a drug to counteract a side effect of another drug. Now do you understand why I suggested maintaining a list of your parent's medications? It can be a nightmare if you are trying to communicate with any of their doctors without knowing what is in your parent's system.

You can find a comprehensive list of drugs used to treat bipolar disorder at http://www.mental-health-today.com. We will look at a few of the more common medications here.

Lithium is a mineral and the most commonly prescribed mood-stabilizing medicine. It has several brand names such as Eskalith, Lithobid, and Lithonate and may be used with other medications such as antipsychotic or antidepressant drugs. It may take weeks or months before lithium takes full effect. Common side effects include weight gain, increased thirst, a frequent need to urinate, trembling, and nausea. Thyroid and kidney problems can occur if the levels of lithium in the blood become too high. That's why it is very important for your parent's levels to be checked on a regular basis.

If your mother or father is experiencing rapid-cycling, their psychiatrist may prescribe Depakote, which is an anti-seizure medication that is also very effective for controlling mania. Common side effects of Depakote include stomach cramps, diarrhea, indigestion, nausea, weight gain, sleepiness, and trembling of the hands. The drug can cause inflammation of the liver and can decrease the amount of platelets needed for the blood to clot. Other anti-seizure medicines that have proven effective in treating bipolar include Tegretol, Lamictal, Neurontin, Lamotrigine, Gabapentin, Topiramate and Topamax.

While anti-depressant drugs such as Prozac, Sertraline (Zoloft®), Bupropion (Wellbutrin®), Venlafaxine (Effexor®) or Paxil are very effective in relieving depression, treating bipolar disorder with antidepressants alone can push a person into a manic state or increase the risk of suicidal thinking and behavior. Anti-depressants are used many times in addition to lithium and other medications to treat bipolar symptoms.

Medications are used to treat bipolar disorder at two levels. One is to control severe symptoms that need immediate attention such as depression, suicidal thoughts, or psychotic behaviors. Known as "acute phase" medications, these include mood-stabilizers such as Lithium, Valproate, Carbamazepine, Lamotrigine, Seroquel and Olanzapine. The other level of treatment is for long-term effects of the disorder or for prevention of future episodes of mania or depression. These chronic phase medications also include Lithium, Valproate, and Carbamazepine given in smaller doses than during an acute phase.

Psychotherapy

Psychotherapy will help your mother or father process consequences of past episodes, manage stress, and improve social functioning. While medication is an extremely effective treatment for bipolar disorder, it's just the beginning. Your parent will also need to work with a therapist so they have an objective third party with whom to talk. My mother recently said that she didn't share a lot of her feelings with her loved ones because she felt we would get upset or wouldn't be able to listen. She made a good point. Because we are so close to her, we may react in a way that doesn't provide her with the most assistance. Individual and group psychotherapy are effective methods of helping your parent deal with any fears, sadness, frustrations, or emotional issues that arise. These methods will likely increase their adherence to drug regimens, enhance their ability to handle social and work situations, decrease their tendency toward denial, and encourage acceptance of their illness.

One psychotherapeutic technique that has proven very effective in treating depression is eye movement desensitization and reprocessing (EMDR). Practitioners use this eight-phase approach to help patients resolve emotional wounds and enable them to replace negative memories or belief systems with preferred positive beliefs. You can find detailed information regarding the process at http://www.emdr.com.

Cognitive therapy is an educational style of treatment that

is effective for patients willing and able to take an active role in modifying their behavior. Cognitive therapy uses a problem-solving approach to help a person identify and correct his or her thinking processes that are producing negative or painful feelings.

In the first chapter, I mentioned that my mother underwent multiple electroconvulsive therapy or ECT treatments. ECT is a technique that has been around nearly a half century and has stirred some controversy over the years. The application of ECT involves using electrical stimulus on the brain to create a seizure, which is believed to jump-start the production of neurotransmitters. When I learned that my mother had received these treatments, I remember thinking, "She must be in bad shape to allow herself to be subjected to such a severe treatment." It has always felt like a last resort treatment to me. Although it was used in the past to control unruly patients, ECT is now used for people with severe depression, suicidal tendencies, or who aren't responding to other treatments. Tests have shown that it is very effective in relieving acute depression because the results are fast (several days). The consistent side effect is loss of memory. My mother, for example, has lost quite a bit of her memory. She isn't a vegetable by any means and her memory loss doesn't prevent her from functioning, but it's a constant frustration for her. When she gets confused, loses her sense of direction, or forgets what she is about to say, I wonder how much of it is caused by her current treatments or from the ECT she received many years ago. All I will say is that it seems to be a viable option, but you may first want to look closely at other alternatives for your parent, if possible.

Tools

More and more people have begun to take control of their own health care. As a result, several effective tools have been developed by people with bipolar to help others manage their illness. In her book, *Loving Someone with Bipolar Disorder*, Julie Fast encourages bipolar people to create a personal treatment plan. Ms. Fast struggled with symptoms for many years before receiving the appropriate diagnosis. Her plan instructs the partner or family member of a bipolar loved one to assist them in taking an inventory of symptoms and triggers specific to the individual; and then, to create a list of statements or activities that have worked well in the past to ease or shorten the phases. The plan might include steps that ensure the bipolar person is taking their meds properly. Their support team may create a checklist of activities that help lower stress such as a nature walk or a massage. The caregivers might include reminders to watch for symptoms or to be aware that the bipolar person has experienced an event (stress, illness, or disturbing news) that could trigger an episode. Many people have been able to stabilize severe moods, minimize or prevent relapses, and control cycling by integrating the personal treatment plan into their overall program that includes prescribed medication and psychotherapy.

Another helpful tool that my mother has used is mood charting. Especially when her psychiatrist is "tweaking" her meds, she tracks her mood on a daily basis to see if any patterns or changes occur. Any significant shifts usually indicate the onset of another episode. The tool is very useful for her doctor in determining the effect of changes in her medication. My mother typically rates her mood on a scale of one to ten—one indicating she is depressed and ten representing manic. There is also an excellent interactive version of mood charting online at http://www.moodswingscontrol.com/product.aspx that allows for complex comparative readings within a date range. The program checks for weight gain, severity of symptoms, sex drive, medication-to-mood ratio, menstrual and biological cycles, sleep patterns, and much more.

Natural Remedies and Therapies

In addition to traditional medicine, many people have found effective natural remedies to control their mood swings. Therapies such as massage, Reiki, and acupuncture are being used as tools for calming and balancing the body.

A non-prescription herbal alternative called ClarocetNRI

is a natural reuptake inhibitor designed to enhance the production and availability of neurotransmitters. ClarocetNRI provides short-term (8-12 hours) relief from nervousness, anxiety, panic, mood fluctuation, irritability, and stress. Other benefits include rapid relaxation of the central nervous system; a more sociable state of mind; a heightening of the senses; a more restful, refreshing sleep; a greater sense of "being in control;" an increased ability to face day-to-day situations and cope with them more effectively; more fulfilling relationships and an overall sense of emotional well-being. One issue with ClarocetNRI is that it contains ingredients that are not compatible with anti-depressant medications.

There are several other natural products on the market, such as BeCalm'd and Serenity (TM), that make similar claims as ClarocetNRI. While these products may be worth further investigation, I strongly suggest that your parent talk with their doctor or pharmacist before taking them with other medications. I do not recommend that anyone stop taking his or her prescribed medications in lieu of this, or any other, herbal supplement.

Light therapy has been proven effective for treating sleep disorders, bipolar, and depression disorders. It is especially helpful for those suffering with winter depression or Seasonal Affective Disorder (SAD) caused by a lack of sunlight. Researchers at Baker Heart Research Institute in Melbourne, Australia found that a person's serotonin levels are higher on bright sunny days regardless of the time of year. These scientists also noted that the amount of serotonin present in the brain reflected the hours of sun exposure on a particular day. Since it is not possible for every SAD patient to fly south for the winter, light therapy provides a more realistic alternative to obtain the healing benefits of light. Simply sit or work under a 10,000-lux, full-spectrum, non-UV light box or SAD lamp for one to two hours a day during times of scarce natural light.

Omega-3 fatty acids (also known as polyunsaturated fatty acids or PUFAs) help nerve cells communicate with each other.

PUFAs play a crucial role in signaling molecules in the body and are essential components of a healthy brain cell membrane. Since the body does not produce them, PUFAa must be obtained from food such as fish and certain plant oils. People who do not maintain a proper balance of PUFAs in their diet are at an increased risk for depression. Omega-3 fatty acids play a role in attention and cognitive abilities like memory, response time, vigilance, and mood. As a result, PUFA supplements may be appropriate for people whose bodies cannot tolerate conventional psychiatric medications.

A lot has been written about the role of amino acids in the treatment of bipolar disorder. The best book I've read on the subject is *The Mood Cure* by Julia Ross. Her holistic approach to supplementing medication with vitamins, minerals, and amino acids makes sense. Research indicates a number of supplements may be beneficial for those with bipolar disorder.

The brain is the most nutritionally sensitive organ in the body. It is constantly producing serotonin, dopamine, norepinephrine, and other chemicals. In order to function properly, the brain depends on nutrients that can be categorized into amino acids, vitamins, and minerals.

An amino acid is an organic compound containing an amino and a carboxyl group. People suffering from depression and bipolar disorder may be totally depleted of these vital nutrients. Amino acids carry messages from cell to cell through the nervous system, and our bodies use amino acids to form the proteins which build muscles, bones, skin, hair, internal organs, and fluids. There are about twenty natural amino acids; some are essential and others are nonessential. The body is unable to manufacture essential amino acids; therefore, your body must get them through your diet. The amino acid supplements that are beneficial in treating bipolar symptoms include L-Tyrosine, Taurine, GABA, L-Tryptophan, Phenylalanine, SAM-e, and 5-Hydroxytryptophan or 5-HTP. Of course, there are additional supplements that are beneficial to your overall health. I suggest taking a look at *The Mood Cure* for details.

The purpose of listing the supplements is to let you know that there are additional treatments available. As I stated before, I am not suggesting that your parent stop taking their prescription medications in lieu of vitamins, minerals or any other supplement or treatment plan. I strongly suggest discussing these supplements with a doctor prior to integrating them into a treatment program.

Research and New Technology

It may be comforting to know that there is a lot of research currently being conducted to better understand, diagnose, and treat bipolar disorder. Some methods are still being evaluated and perfected. Many of the technologies are still awaiting approval for use in the United States. Here are some of the newer techniques and findings.

Vagus Nerve Stimulation for Depression

If your parent is not responding to treatment for depression, there is a new technology called Vagus Nerve Stimulation (VNS) that has proven effective for patients who experience recurrent treatment-resistant depression. The vagus nerve carries information to the region of the brain believed to be responsible for seizures, mood, appetite, and anxiety. Through a small surgically implanted wire attached to a pulse generator in the chest, VNS prompts changes in neurotransmitters by delivering a miniscule electrical pulse to the left cervical vagus nerve in the neck.

VNS has commonly been used to treat epilepsy. When clinical trial participants also reported an improvement in mood, researchers created a separate trial for patients with severe depression. The pilot study reported that participants displayed a fifty percent improvement in their mood. Several patients improved so much they were able to return to work or resume normal activities, and have continued to do well.

VNS technology is safe and does not cause the side effects normally associated with ECT or depression medications. The most recent information indicated that VNS with the Cyberonics' NCP System had been approved for sale in the European Union and in Canada, and was still pending FDA approval in the United States.

Transcranial Magnetic Stimulation

Transcranial Magnetic Stimulation (TMS) is a non-invasive method of applying a focal current to the cerebral cortex of the brain to ease the symptoms of depression and other disorders. A figure-eight-shaped wand with two coils of wire is placed near the patient's head. The coils generate a strong magnetic field that induces electrical currents in brain cells, which are believed to normalize disturbed levels of brain activity. TMS is an outpatient procedure that does not require anesthesia and does not affect memory or cause seizures. While TMS devices have received FDA approval as diagnostic tools for mood disorders, more research is needed to determine its long-term effectiveness as a therapeutic procedure. A TMS device manufactured by NeoPulse, a U.S. company, has received approval in Canada and Israel as a therapy for depression.

Echo-Planer Magnetic Resonance Spectroscopic Imaging

Using Echo-Planer Magnetic Resonance Spectroscopic Imaging, (EP-MRSI), Harvard Medical School researchers were trying to determine how the brain chemistry and nerve cell activity of bipolar patients differs from that of non-bipolar people. Immediately after the scan, participants said they felt more cheerful than before and continued to feel the effects for as long as a week. Surprised by their accidental discovery, the researchers decided to investigate further to see if electromagnetic fields generated by the scanner could actually nudge a depressed brain back toward normal. In the new study, they selected a mix of bipolar and non-bipolar participants. Some of the test participants were given the EP-MRSI while others underwent "sham scans" to test the placebo effect. The results were amazing. Seventy-seven percent of the people with bipolar depression felt better after the EP-MRSI scanning than before the procedure. The results suggest that electromagnetic pulses may restore balance in the two halves of the brain, which are out of balance during depression.

The EP-MRSI scanners are large enough to fill a room and cost millions of dollars, so they are not a very practical treatment tool yet. However, work has begun on the design of a smaller, less expensive device that may someday allow patients to ease their depression during a 20-minute nap in a doctor's office. So far, the scanning technique seems free of side effects.

One Medication for the Ups and Downs

As I mentioned earlier, my mother is on six different medications for the treatment of her disorder—and one of them is to counter side effects from one of those very drugs. It never occurred to me that there could actually be one medication that addressed all aspects of bipolar. The mania and the depression have always been treated separately, but there is now a drug called Seroquel that can treat both. Seroquel is an antipsychotic medication currently used to treat acute mania on a short-term basis. Two separate tests of the drug were conducted at the Bipolar Research Center at University Hospital of Cleveland and Case Western Reserve University School of Medicine. The results of these two tests showed a reduction in suicidal thoughts of bipolar I and II patients. Although Seroquel is currently licensed in the United States to treat only mania symptoms, the results of the tests should prompt the manufacturer to pursue FDA approval for its use in the treatment of bipolar depression as well.

Treatment for bipolar disorder is not just about taking pills everyday. While some form of medication, whether it be manufactured or natural, is required to treat the disease, there are additional therapies required for a bipolar person to lead a full, healthy life. It is important that your parent work with their health care team to maintain a well-rounded program that ensures their optimum mental, emotional, and physical health.

Although it feels like a snail's pace, these new treatments and technologies continue to move forward and be improved. Who knows? Maybe soon we'll have a blood test or a brain scan that can detect or rule out bipolar disorder. Maybe some day a person's brain chemistry can be analyzed so their doctor can prescribe just the right mix of drugs that will stabilize their condition within days. Maybe there will be a program of natural substances that prove even more effective than the manufactured drugs or maybe one medication, like Seroquel, will be approved to effectively and safely treat mania as well as depression. Maybe a day will come when corporations openly discuss mental illness and provide employee training to eliminate the stigma. I believe it can all be done, but it is not up to the mental health practitioners. It's up to us and our parents to explore and communicate. As you discover new treatments, share them with people in your support group or find a place to post them on the Internet. Together we can bring visibility to bipolar disorder and how to help our loved ones.

Chapter 23

It's About Acceptance

Looking at your life may not have been pleasant. It may have caused you to feel sad or angry and taken you to some scary places. I truly hope you were able to recall some of your joy as well. Regardless of your journey, it's important that you know your life can now be what you want it to be. Your parent, spouse, job, or preacher is not in charge of your life. You are in charge of choosing your path and deciding what you want it to be. I challenge you to *accept* your power, voice your needs, and establish healthy boundaries.

Accept your parent's diagnosis. While your parent's acceptance of their diagnosis is most critical, your own belief is also very important. That's not to say you should blindly accept any diagnosis, but observe your parent as he or she begins the treatments. If you see a leveling out of their mood swings, you'll know the diagnosis is correct. Do whatever is necessary to release your own negativity regarding bipolar disorder and mental illness. Remember that your parent is not intentionally trying to ruin their life or yours. Once I understood that my mother's behavior did not always reflect her true character and that it was related to her illness, I was able to forgive her past choices and the impact they had on me. I still had to work through the resulting challenges, but building a healthy relationship with my mother has been a tremendous gift that came from that forgiveness.

Accept the truth about bipolar disorder. You needn't feel

ashamed about your parent's diagnosis. Scientists have proven that the chemistry in your mother or father's brain is different from a person who does not experience severe emotional highs and lows. How would you feel if your parent had been diagnosed with heart disease instead of bipolar disorder? Medically, there is no difference because each is a result of dis-ease in the body. Would you be embarrassed to say your parent had diabetes? The only difference is the stigma people hold about mental illness, which stems from lack of understanding.

The sooner you can *accept* that your mother/father is not capable of being emotionally supportive, the sooner you can create a stronger support system for yourself. You are worthy of that emotional support and you can find it within yourself. I'm not suggesting that you isolate yourself and not look to others for support. I simply mean that you needn't rely completely on the people around you. Otherwise, you risk giving your life over to them and not making the choices that ensure happiness in *your* life.

Accept the genius of bipolar. Because bipolar disorder is so prevalent, there are people in every profession generating the most creative and globally transforming work conceivable. These are the same people whose relationships, schoolwork, research, jobs, and quality of life are disrupted by a chemical imbalance. Most of them are not famous. They are hard-working family members, friends, and coworkers.

Some people want to find a cure for it, but think of what our world would be like without bipolar disorder. Dr. Kay Redfield Jamison, professor of psychiatry at Johns Hopkins University, submits that there is value in this "disease" of the brain. Some of the world's most intelligent and imaginative individuals are/were bipolar. You may be surprised to know that the following people have been diagnosed with bipolar disorder (either retrospectively or currently):

U.S. Presidents	Abraham Lincoln Theodore Roosevelt
Composers/Musicians	George Handel Robert Schumann Ludwig van Beethoven Charles Mingus Peter Gabriel Charlie Pride
Writers	Virginia Woolf Ernest Hemingway Cole Porter Charles Dickens
Poets	Sylvia Plath Hart Crane
Physicist	Sir Issac Newton
Actors	Patty Duke Linda Hamilton
Artists	Michelangelo Vincent van Gogh Georgia O'Keefe
Society Leaders	Winston Churchill Ted Turner Kitty Dukakis
TV Hosts	Jane Pauley Dick Cavett

Try to imagine our world without the contributions these people have made. They produced legendary music, rendered beautiful works of art, changed society through their leadership, and revolutionized cultures with their visionary efforts despite the peaks and valleys of bipolar. I'm not aware of any scientific studies to prove it, but maybe the manic surge of ideas and energy is the thing that sets these history makers apart from the rest of the world. Think about your own parent during manic phases. My mother created the most incredible clothing, jewelry, and other crafts during her high times. She could work on projects for days without needing or wanting to stop for any reason. She was able to comprehend complex accounting problems and absorb mass amounts of information.

A very dear friend of mine is a teacher and counselor. While working at a recent seminar, he was called to an attendee's hotel room. The young man greeted my friend in his dress slacks and no shirt. My friend was taken back by the sight of the young man's room. He had moved all the furniture into one corner. His bathroom mirror was covered with complex mathematical formulas. He implored my friend to help him build an energy source by placing jumbo paper clips around the bottom of a lamp shade. The young man had been very polite and friendly with other attendees. Apparently, something he experienced during the seminar triggered his manic episode. He was not violent in any way, but his behavior was foreign to those around him. The next day he was diagnosed with bipolar disorder and began the typical treatment program.

I was sad for this young man—not because he was bipolar. I was saddened because of the shame I knew his family was feeling and because he would never be the same. He will struggle because he is now caught between two worlds—our world and his new world that is full of ideas, possibilities, and information.

I believe the future is bright for those affected by bipolar disorder. Understanding and love are the keys to that future— understanding the impact of the disease and love for those affected—including ourselves. I ask that you become part of creating a shift in consciousness by sharing information and educating people about bipolar disorder. Let go of your shame and talk about your experience. You'll be surprised at the number of people who will be able to relate to you. Through the strength of our knowledge and unity of purpose we can make a better life for ourselves and those we love.

Appendix A

Resources for Bipolar Disorder

1. American Psychiatric Association, 1400 K Street NW, Washington, DC 20005, (703) 907-7300, http://www.psych.org.

2. bp Magazine, P.O. Box 59, Buffalo, NY 14205-0059, (866) 672-3038, http://www.bphope.com.

3. Depression and Bipolar Support Alliance (DBSA), 730 N. Franklin, Suite 501, Chicago, IL 60610 (800) 826-3632, http://www.dbsalliance.org.

4. Foundations Associates, Recovery Resource Hotline (800) 575-4605, www.dualdiagnosis.org.

5. Mood Tracking device: http://www.moodswingscontrol.com/

6. National Alliance for the Mentally Ill (NAMI), 200 North Glebe Road, Suite 1015, Arlington, VA 22203-3754 (800) 950-NAMI, http://www.nami.org/

7. National Institute of Mental Health (NIMH), Information Resources and Inquiries Branch, Room 7C-02, 5600 Fishers Lane, Rockville, MD 20857, (866) 615-6464, http://www.nimh.nih.gov.

8. National Mental Health Association (NMHA), 2001

N. Beauregard Street, 12th Floor, Alexandria, Virginia 22311, (800) 969-6642, http://www.nmha.org.

9. National Mental Health Consumer Self-Help Clearinghouse. 1211 Chestnut Street, Suite 1207, Philadelphia, PA 19107, (800) 553-4539, http://www.mhselfhelp.org/.

10. National Mental Health Public Awareness Campaign, (202) 778-2309.

Appendix B

Bipolar Disorder Support Groups

Depression and Bipolar Support Alliance (DBSA) 730 N. Franklin Street, Suite 501, Chicago, IL 60610-7224. www. DBSAlliance.org (800) 826-3632.

Dr. John Grohol's Psych Central; Online Bipolar Community: http://psychcentral.com/resources/Bipolar/Support_Groups/

Dual Recovery Anonymous http://draonline.org/meetings

Healthy Place — Bipolar Community; Support Group Calendar: http://www.healthyplace.com/communities/bipolar/ site/comm_calender.htm

Tuft's University Child & Family Web Guide; Resources: http://www.cfw.tufts.edu/topic/5/116.htm.

Works Cited

1. "A Brief Description of EMDR." EMDR Institute, Inc. 22 June 2005.

2. http://www.emdr.com/briefdes.htm

3. "About Trauma Dissociative Disorders." Sidran Foundation 28 Jan. 2005. http://www.sidran.org/didbr.html

4. "Amino Acids" BPhoenix Advice Columns 20 June 2005. http://www.angelfire.com/home/bphoenix1/amino.html

5. "Author's Family Hopes to End Stigma." USA Today 8 March 2005. http://www.usatoday.com/life/people/2005-03-07-chang-family_x.htm?POE=LIFISVA

6. "Bipolar Disorder" Health Notes 20 June 2005. http://www.gnc.com/health_notes/healthnotes.aspx?ContentID=1167002&lang=en

7. "Bipolar Disorder Research at the National Institute of Mental Health." National Institute of Mental Health 18 January 2005. http://www.nimh.nih.gov/publicat/bipolarresfact.cfm

8.   "Bipolar Disorder." MentalHealth-Go Beyond the Thought 22 March 2005. http://www.imentalhealth.com/bipolar/

9.   "Common Myths, The Truth About Bipolar Disorder." Bipolar.com 21 March 2005. http://www.bipolar.com/whatis/myths.htm

10.   "Don't Drink the Diet Coke." McMan's Depression and Bipolar Web 20 June 2005. http://www.mcmanweb.com/article-110.htm

11.   "Evidence of Brain Chemistry Abnormalities in Bipolar Disorder." University of Michigan - General Clinical Research Center Press Release 19 January 2005. http://bipolar.about.com/cs/bpbasics/a/what_causes_bp_2.htm

12.   "Famous Faces and Names with Bipolar Disorder." Manics Dance. 17 March 2005. http://www.mentaljokes.com/famous_manic.html

13.   "Gaps Exist In Public's Understanding Of Bipolar Disorder - National Survey Validates Need for Better Education, Improved Diagnosis." Planetpsych.com A World of Information 21 March 2005. http://www.planetpsych.com/zPsychology_101/gaps_in_understanding.htm

14. "Let's Talk Facts About Mental Illnesses An Overview." American Psychiatric Press 10 February 2005. http://www.psych.org/public_info/hospital.cfm

15. "Mental Disorders" 10 February 2005. Psychiatry 24x7.com http://www.psychiatry24x7.com/bgdisplay.jhtml?itemname=nonprofbackbip015

16. "Myths and FAQs About Mental Illness." Will I Go Crazy? 21 March 2005. http://willigocrazy.org/Ch05c.htm

17. "New Medicines for Mental Health - Help Avert a Spending Crisis." Mental Health Medications (Psychotropics) Today 14 January 2004. http://www.mental-health-today.com/rx/new_meds.htm

18. "New Seroquel data support benefits in bipolar disorder." Medical News Today 29 June 2005. http://www.medicalnewstoday.com/medicalnews.php?newsid=25058

19. "Seasonal Affective Disorder Treatment" Apollo Health 10 February 2005. http://www.apollolight.com/new_content/about_sad/sad1.html

20.   "Selective Serotonin Reuptake Inhibitor"
      Wikipedia, The Free Encyclopedia 1 January
      2005. http://en.wikipedia.org/wiki/Selective_
      serotonin_reuptake_inhibitor#List_of_SSRIs

21.   "The Fundamentals of Mental Health and Mental
      Illness" Mental health: A report of the Surgeon
      General 10 February 2005. http://dev13.shs.net/
      features/surgeongeneralreport/chapter2/sec1.
      asp

22.   "The Mood Disorder Questionnaire" DBSA Web
      site 25 January 2005. http://www.dbsalliance.
      org/questionnaire/screening.asp

23.   "Vagus Nerve Stimulation In Depression."
      Depression Central 8 February 2005. http://www.
      psycom.net/depression.central.vagus.html

24.   "Vagus Nerve Stimulation Successful for
      Depression" Doctor's Guide Global Edition 7
      February 2005. http://www.pslgroup.com/dg/
      15131a.htm

25.   "What are the symptoms of Bipolar Disorder?"
      Bipolar Depression Info 19 January 2005. http://
      www.bipolardepressioninfo.com/ms/guides/
      treat_bipolar_disorder/main.html

26. Bailey, Kimberly "What Causes Bipolar Disorder?" About.com Bipolar Disorder. 18 January 2005. http://bipolar.about.com/cs/bpbasics/a/what_causes_bp.htm

27. Bailey, Kimberly . "Nutritional Supplements: Amino Acids." About.com 20 June 2005. http://bipolar.about.com/cs/menu_nutrition/a/9907_aminoacid.htm

28. Cromie, William J. "Depressed Get a Lift From MRI; Brain Scanners Please Manic-depressives." Harvard Gazette Archives, Harvard News Office 10 February 2005. http://www.news.harvard.edu/gazette/2004/01.22/01-depression.html

29. Fast, Julie A. "Information and Products to Help Children and Adults with Bipolar Disorder Find Relief and Live Life to the Fullest!" Bipolar Happens. 9 January 2005. http://www.bipolarhappens.com.

30. Fast, Julie A. and John D. Preston, PsyD. Loving Someone with Bipolar Disorder, Understanding & Helping Your Partner. California: New Harbinger Publications, Inc. 2004.

31. Goldberg, Ivan, MD. "Goldberg's Depression Scale." Mayo Clinic 25 January 2005. http://www.dragonpack.com/mentalhealth/depression/goldberg.shtml

32. Goldberg, Ivan, MD. "Screening for Bipolar Spectrum Disorders." Mayo Clinic 25 January 2005. http://www.psycom.net/depression.central.bipolar-screening.html

33. Grayson, Charlotte E., MD. "Bipolar Disorder (Manic Depressive Disorder)." Medical Information from the Cleveland Clinic on Web MD Health 11 January 2005. http://my.webmd.com/content/Article/60/67149.htm

34. Jamison, Kay Redfield. Touched with Fire: Manic Depressive Illness and the Artistic Temperament. 1993. The Free Press, a Division of Simon and Schuster. 10 February 2005.

35. Keck, Paul, M.D. University of Cincinnati College of Medicine in an interview with Claire Ginther. Bipolar Disorder FAQs 20 January 2005. http://www.mhsource.com/bipolar/bdfaq.html#2

36. Kelsoe, Dr. John R. "Bipolar Disorder." UCSD Department of Psychiatry Genetics Research Program 20 January 2005. http://www.bipolar. ucsd.edu/Download/Kelsoe%20DBSA%2010- 22-04.ppt

37. Kidder, Margot. "The Role of Amino Acids in Bipolar Disorder and Mental Health." Safe Harbor 20 June 2005. http:// www.alternativementalhealth.com/articles/ aminobipolar.htm

38. Mandel, Debbie Eisenstadt. "Can Caretakers Take Care Of Themselves?" Turn on Your Inner Light 22 March 2005. http://turnonyourinnerlight. com/CanCaretakersTakeCareOfThemselves2. htm

39. Mandel, Debbie Eisenstadt. "How To Deal With Anger - The C.O.P.E Method." Turn on Your Inner Light 22 March 2005. http://turnonyourinnerlight.com/ HowToCopeWithAnger2.htm

40. Mandel, Debbie Eisenstadt. "How to Deal With Anxiety: From Worrier to Warrior." Turn on Your Inner Light 22 March 2005. http://turnonyourinnerlight.com/ HowToDealWithAnxiety.html

41. Mandel, Debbie Eisenstadt. "How to Have a Constructive Conflict." Turn on Your Inner Light 18 March 2005. http://www.turnonyourinnerlight. com/ConstructiveConflict.html

42. Mayo, Julia, MD. "How to Avoid a Manic Episode." Department of Psychiatry, St. Vincent's Hospital 9 February 2005. http://www. bpso.org/nomania.htm

43. McManamy, John. "Nutritional Supplements for Bipolar Disorder." Healthy Place.com 20 June 2005. http://www.healthyplace.com/communities/ bipolar/treatment/alternative/nutritional_ supplements.asp

44. Miklowitz, David J. Ph.D. "Psychoeducational Family Management." 8 February 2005. http:// www.wpic.pitt.edu/stanley/2ndbipconf/ppt/ W404_10/tsld002.htm

45. Miklowitz, David J., PhD. The Bipolar Disorder Survival Guide – What You and Your Family Need to Know. New York: The Guilford Press 2002.

46. Oliver, David. "How To Deal And Cope With Your Loved One's Bipolar Disorder" Bipolar Central 25 January 2005. http://www.leverageteamllc. com/bipolarletter8/

47. Pheil, Tim and Andrea Pheil, L.P.N. Bipolar Disorder Self-Care 20 June 2005. http://www. mhsanctuary.com/bipolar/selfcare.htm

48. Ross, Julia, M.A. The Mood Cure: The 4-Step Program to Take Charge of Your Emotions - Today. 3 June 2005. New York: Penguin Press 2002.

49. SerVaas, Cory, MD. About Bipolar Disorder/ Manic-Depressive Illness. Bipolar Genetics Collaboration. 20 January 2005. http://www. bipolargenes.org/

50. Stoll, Andrew L, M.D. "The Omega-3 Connection: How You Can Restore Your Body's Natural Balance and Treat Depression Chapter One: Nature's Mood Enhancers" Bipolar Central 28 February 2005. http://www.leverageteamllc. com/omega%2D3/

51. Thompson, Dennis. "One Drug Treats Both Sides of Bipolar Disorder." Bipolar Depression Info. 19 January 2005. http://www.bipolardepressioninfo.com/ms/news/518775/main.html

52. Womack, Dr. David S. "The Role of Family and Friends." Highland Avenue Baptist Church 7 February 2005. http://www.habcnc.com/bipolarism.htm49.   Oliver, David. "How To Deal And Cope With Your Loved One's Bipolar Disorder" Bipolar Central 25 January 2005. http://www.leverageteamllc.com/bipolarletter8/